Famous Detectives

True Stories of Great Crime Detection

Books by Eugene B. Block

Famous Detectives

Fifteen Clues

The Wizard of Berkeley

Great Train Robberies of the West

Great Stagecoach Robbers of the West

And May God Have Mercy

The Vindicators

Above the Civil War

Famous Detectives

True Stories of Great Crime Detection

Eugene B. Block

Doubleday & Company, Inc.
Garden City, New York
1967

LIBRARY OF CONGRESS CATALOG CARD NUMBER 67–18238
COPYRIGHT © 1967 BY EUGENE B. BLOCK
PRINTED IN THE UNITED STATES OF AMERICA
FIRST EDITION

To Ruth with love

Acknowledgments

The author, with a deep sense of gratitude, extends his profoundest thanks to the many people in various parts of the United States and overseas whose assistance made this book possible. They include:

Federal Bureau of Investigation, Washington, D.C.

Warden E. L. Maxwell, Ohio State Penitentiary, Columbus, Ohio

Schindler Bureau of Investigation, New York City

Andre Euloge, Paris, France

John J. McCloy, New York City

E. Spencer Shew CBE, London, England

William H. Stone, chief special agent, Southern Pacific Railroad, San Francisco, Calif.

Inspector Tamegoro Ikii, Tokyo, Japan

George Somekawa, Tokyo, Japan

Kimpei Shiba, Tokyo, Japan

Bryant Hall, San Francisco, Calif.

James L. Adams, Cincinnati, Ohio

Col. George Hunter White, San Francisco, Calif.

Ray F. Hyland, New York City

Richard Sloane, New York City

William J. Burns National Detective Agency, New York City

Edgar T. Gleeson, Mill Valley, Calif.

David A. Goode, New York City

Pinkerton's National Detective Agency, New York City

M. Russell Moyer, Pinkerton Agency, San Francisco, Calif.

Arnold Harris, Washington, D.C.

The late Arthur M. Johnson, San Mateo, Calif.

Harland Manchester, New York City

Howard Imazaki, San Francisco, Calif.

Judge Donald B. Constine, San Francisco, Calif.

Contents

Famous Detectives

True Stories of Great Crime Detection

Chapter 1

America's Pioneer Detective
Allan Pinkerton

Gloom hung heavily over the once placid, contented town of Atkinson, Mississippi.* It was early spring 1855 and nearly four months had passed since one of its most popular young men had been brutally murdered in a bank and its vault looted of nearly $130,000 in gold and currency. Despite the efforts of local and state police, aided by private detectives, not a single tangible clue had been uncovered.

Aside from an urge to see justice done, the townspeople were restless and nervous, fearing that the killers were members of a gang from another state and would return.

At the bank two factors contributed to mounting tension. Not only were the officials worried over so heavy a financial loss, but there were very personal and emotional reasons why they wanted to see the crime avenged. The victim, George Gordon, had been a favorite among his colleagues and the idolized nephew of the vice-president, Peter A. Gordon, who had raised him as a son.

After long weeks of disappointment, Alexander Bannintine, the bank president, had come forward with a new proposal. "I've been thinking that we ought to send for Allan Pinkerton," he said. "He's the shrewdest detective in the country and he's done some remarkable things—catching

---

* Reporting this case in his memoirs some years later, Pinkerton noted that the names of the town and some of the characters were fictitious to spare relatives of the culprit still residing in the area.

other bank robbers, tracking Jesse James and the Reno brothers for train holdups. He might just be able to help us here."

His associates agreed and Thomas McGregor, cashier of the City Bank of Atkinson, undertook to contact the pioneer detective.

Pinkerton received the message in his Chicago office just as he was clearing his desk preparatory to a short vacation. The case interested him and after some thought he decided to accept the assignment, though he was tired and needed rest. He advised the bankers that he would leave for Mississippi in a few days and communicate with them from there as soon as possible after his arrival. He told them the fictitious name that he would assume, explaining that he intended to pose as a wealthy cotton speculator which would give him plausible reason to visit the bank without attracting undue attention. Working in a day when scientific means of crime detection were practically unknown, Pinkerton followed methods of his own. This time he wanted no one in the town to suspect that the stranger might be a detective.

Arriving in Atkinson, he spent the day familiarizing himself with his new surroundings, exchanging pleasantries with prominent citizens in the hotel, and casually discussing the cotton market. Not until early evening did he communicate with the bank president, who suggested that he enter the bank through a little-used private doorway.

Shortly afterward he was greeted by Bannintine who introduced McGregor and the vice-president, Peter A. Gordon, who chose to open the conversation.

"I loved my nephew George as if he were my own son," he began with some emotion. "He was the only son of my brother who was drowned twenty years ago, and I raised George from babyhood. Personally, I don't care how much we spend if we can find whoever killed him."

Pinkerton interrupted to ask for all of the facts in the

case and as the bankers took turns in talking, he frequently jotted words and phrases in his notebook.

George Gordon, he was told, was an unusual young man of twenty-five, as efficient as he was earnest about his work, always thinking first of duty and caring little for pleasures. During his five years as paying teller, he had won the respect of the bank's influential clients.

He often had returned to his desk at night and occasionally he would accommodate a belated customer knocking on the door to cash a check or to make a deposit.

At this point Gordon suggested that he relate the events immediately preceding and following the crime, for both Bannintine and McGregor had been away on business. "George had left the bank soon after closing time," his uncle stated, "and we both dined together at the hotel as we usually did. George told me he was returning here to finish up some work and . . ."

"Do you know anyone who met him here that night?" Pinkerton interrupted.

"Only one man—a jeweler named Flanders," Gordon answered. "Flanders usually came in late with a box of valuables to store overnight in the vault. He tells me that this night George simply took the box and walked away, explaining that he was too busy for conversation. We have found no one else who talked to George after that."

Gordon then related that a short time after ten the following morning, while he was in a store, a man informed him that the bank was still closed. Suspecting that George Gordon had been taken ill, his uncle hastened to the bank and found a small group of excited people milling about the entrance. After first trying the front doors and finding them locked, he had hurried to the private entrance, giving the secret signal—three short, quick knocks. When this brought no answer, the banker tried the door and to his surprise it swung open.

Hurrying inside, he had not gone far in the unlighted

place when he stumbled against something on the floor. Before him was the crumpled body of his nephew, lying in a pool of blood midway between his own desk and the open vault. His head was badly battered. Furniture and walls were spattered with reddish stains. Near the body lay a heavy canceling hammer, covered with blood and matted hair, obviously the murder weapon.

Suspecting robbery, the terrified banker first called police and then the coroner. When the body was lifted from the floor, it was seen that the dead man's hand still clutched a $100 bill.

Turning now to details of the early inquiry, Gordon stated that the police had discovered remnants of clothing and papers burned in the bank's fireplace, which had been cleaned the day before. He handed Pinkerton a few buttons taken from the charred debris, together with two small pieces of paper. One had been twisted to light the fire and was partly burned. The other, bloodstained, with penciled numbers on one side, had been found under the body. Pinkerton put these aside, saying that he would examine them later.

He then inquired about the bank's loss and was told by Gordon that Bannintine and McGregor, notified of the murder, had hurried back to Atkinson, arriving in the afternoon. Checking their loss, they had found that $105,000 in currency was missing, together with $23,000 in gold coin. Two $20 pieces had been picked up a few days later by a slave on the bank of Rocky Creek, a short distance out of town. This had led to a belief that robbers might be hiding in the woods but a careful search had failed.

The banker added that two bundles of old checks and paid-up notes had been taken from the vault and used to start the fire but the local police had disregarded this as unimportant.

Pinkerton at this point stated that he wished to ask some questions and he first inquired who, besides the jeweler,

Flanders, came to the bank at night. Several prominent citizens were named, including the county clerk, Alexander Drysdale, who occasionally dropped in late to deposit last-minute fees.

With an interest that obviously puzzled the bankers, Pinkerton asked about each man who had been named. He was assured that all of them were influential citizens, none of whom needed money. "They're all successful men like Drysdale, the county clerk," Bannintine interjected. "He was really one of George's closest friends. This thing upset him so that he refused to be foreman of the coroner's jury. He said he just couldn't take it."

The same group of men, Bannintine explained, knew where George Gordon hid the vault keys; they also knew the secret signal by which he admitted them at night. No others had this information.

After further talk, Pinkerton reached for the two small sheets of paper he had put aside and examined them carefully in silence. He pursed his lips and the bank officials inquired anxiously whether he had found a clue. The detective shrugged his shoulders and merely asked if he could take the papers and the buttons with him. "I'd like to study them for a day or two—alone—by myself," he said.

In the quiet and seclusion of his hotel room Pinkerton spent hours over the two little pieces of paper—the blood-stained one found under the body, and the charred piece taken from the fireplace. The more he studied them the more puzzled he became.

On one side of the stained sheet he found faintly penciled numbers, one row under the other, as if the writer had added and subtracted. He finally turned to the second paper, gazed at it for a time, and whistled softly. It was the charred fragment of a note for $927.78 and it bore a signature: *Alexander P. Drysdale.*

His curiosity thoroughly aroused, Pinkerton lit his desk lamp and closely scrutinized the paper for a date. The day and month had been burned away but by holding the note in a bright light at a certain angle he was able to discern the figures of the current year, 1855.

Eagerly he picked up his pencil and spent the next hour in mathematics. Near midnight he sent a message to Bannintine, requesting a meeting early the next evening. He said that he would be occupied during the day but that the meeting he requested was of great importance.

Pinkerton arose early the next morning, conversed in the hotel lobby about land prices, and finally made his way to Drysdale's office. "I'm anxious to buy a good plantation," he told the county clerk. "You might hear of someone who wants to sell."

Drysdale, a handsome man in his middle forties, said that a friend, whose property adjoined his own plantation, was anxious to sell. "Write his name down for me," the detective asked. "My memory isn't very good."

Pinkerton tucked the little piece of paper in his vest pocket, said he would return at another time, and walked away.

That night he found the bankers awaiting him with eager curiosity. "Have you found a clue?" Bannintine inquired anxiously.

Pinkerton's weathered face broke into a wry smile. "Maybe so—and then maybe not," he answered. "It depends very largely on some information that I need from you. If my reckoning is correct, it just may be that poor George Gordon wrote the name of his murderer for us to see."

The others stared at him with blank astonishment but before they could ask for an explanation, he asked two pointed questions:

"First, I want to know the bank balances of Flanders, Drysdale, and the others you have mentioned—those prominent men who came around here at night. And secondly, that burned paper they took from the fireplace—could it have fallen out of those bundles of old checks and notes that were taken from the vault and burned?"

As to the note, the bankers were certain that it had slipped out from one of the bundles. Replying to the first question Bannintine opened his books which showed that each of the men in question had a considerable balance in his account, though Drysdale's was the lowest—$324.22.

Pinkerton wrote the figure on a sheet of paper and silently undertook some calculations while the others watched him curiously. When he had finished he looked up and his eyes were shining.

"Exactly what are you getting at?" one of the bankers inquired, but Pinkerton said that at this time he preferred to answer them with a hypothetical question. "Just let us suppose," he began, "and I emphasize the word *suppose*, that a man of prominence needs money in a hurry—a small amount. He goes to his bank at night and a friend agrees to lend him what he needs. He signs a note and his friend opens the vault to get the money. The customer suddenly sees before him large bundles of currency. A sudden insane frenzy overtakes him. 'All that money,' he tells himself, 'and I'm only getting a paltry sum.' In that state of mind he succumbs to a crazy impulse; he kills his friend, gathers up the money, and burns his bloody clothes. Now I ask you, gentlemen, could that be possible?"

The bankers nodded, pressing for an explanation. Pinkerton drew his chair closer to the others and asked them to inspect the charred note and the paper on which he had been calculating. "First, gentlemen," he told them, "you will notice that this note is dated in the current year. It's signed by Alexander Drysdale. It couldn't have dropped from the old bundles in the vault because if it had been paid it would have been canceled and returned to the maker. Now I ask you to look first at the figures on this burned note— $927.78; then examine these penciled numbers that I found on that paper which lay under George's body."

The men rose to their feet, read the figures, and urged Pinkerton to continue.

"Here it is," Pinkerton went on, "and I ask you to follow me very closely. The penciled numbers show the subtraction of $324.22 from $1252 and the difference, $927.78—the precise sum written on the note. And $324.22 is Drysdale's bank balance as you just told me. I'm sure you don't need to be detectives to reckon what happened. Drysdale, one of the few men admitted to the bank at night, evidently called to borrow $1252. Obviously, George agreed to give it to him but deducted the current balance, which gives us the exact amount written on the note. Simple, isn't it?"

For a few moments the astonished bankers could not speak but before they regained their composure the detective resumed. "Today I used a ruse to get Drysdale to write in my presence. He's left-handed. Remember, the coroner told you that all of the blows on George's head were on the left side. And then . . ."

"Why in the world wasn't all this discovered before?" Bannintine interrupted.

"I'll tell you why," the detective was quick to answer. "Most investigators make the mistake of looking first for the culprit and making the evidence fit him. I do just the reverse. Now, gentlemen, we have the culprit and some of the evidence—but far from enough to warrant an arrest, much less to convince a jury. I ask your permission to have Drysdale shadowed. My procedure will depend on what we learn; it'll be slow work but I am very hopeful."

With their full consent to this proposal, Pinkerton returned to Chicago, sent for one of his shrewdest men, Timothy Webster, and instructed him to go at once to Atkinson and report to him daily or even more often if circumstances warranted. To assist him a clever woman detective, Mrs. Kate Warne, and a young man named Green were dispatched to Mississippi but they were not to arrive together.

A week later, Webster, immaculately dressed and with the air of a prosperous merchant, walked into the Atkinson hotel and registered as John M. Andrews of Baltimore. He saw to it that he met other guests and let it be known that he had come to buy a business.

In a few days the hotel had another new guest, a fashionably gowned woman of apparent refinement and culture. She presented herself as Mrs. R. C. Potter and said she was a widow from Florida looking for new surroundings. Nothing about her indicated that she was traveling under an assumed name or that she had come for a very different purpose.

Mrs. Potter made friends easily. Soon she was asked to accompany several women of the town on a walk. They told her that she must meet a Mrs. Drysdale, one of their most popular clubwomen, and introductions followed. Drysdale returned home while the women were chatting in the parlor and after joining in their conversation he finally remarked that he hoped Mrs. Potter would call on his wife while he was out of town.

"I didn't know you were going away," Mrs. Drysdale said with some surprise.

"Only for a few days, my dear," he told her. "There's a man here at the hotel from Baltimore named Andrews. I'm taking him out to the plantation. He might buy our neighbor's place. A nice sort of chap. Mrs. Potter, have you met him?"

"Just casually," said Mrs. Potter with little apparent interest.

Next day, as Andrews and Drysdale, traveling together, reined their horses so that they could converse, a friendship soon developed and the county clerk said that he hoped the newcomer might become his neighbor.

Some nights later Mrs. Potter and Andrews "chanced" to dine together. Andrews told her that Pinkerton, still in Chicago, was disappointed and impatient; for him the case was moving far too slowly. He had expected that by this time a definite plan to trap the suspect would have been evolved.

"So what do we do now?" Mrs. Potter inquired, obviously worried.

"For one thing," Andrews answered, "I'm going to pay a personal call on that man Breed who runs the carpenter shop here in town. All the old-timers gather in his place to gossip. That's why I had our young investigator, Green, get himself a job there, just so he'd have a chance to overhear what was being said about the case but Green hasn't picked up a single word worthwhile. So I'm going to buzz Breed myself on some pretext. Maybe I can pry something out of the old buzzard."

Andrews arose early the next morning and walked hopefully to the carpenter shop but he little thought that by a strange circumstance a supposedly casual remark by Breed would point the way to new and daring strategy that ultimately would solve the case.

In the shop Andrews introduced himself and asked Breed where he could find a cabinetmaker. "I need someone to put together a cheap little bookcase for my room," he explained.

"I know just the man for you," Breed answered quickly. "A young fellow from Memphis who's been doing odd jobs here in the shop for me. He's handy; I'll send him around."

This, of course, was Andrews' simple way of establishing contact with Breed. He had reckoned in advance that he would need some reason to turn the conversation to the murder and, to this end, he had asked Gordon, the banker, to walk slowly by Breed's place at the exact time that Andrews would be there.

Just as Andrews was about to leave the shop, he spied the banker outside and waved to him. "There goes Gordon walking by," the detective commented casually. "Wonder if he'll ever hear anything about that murder."

Breed shrugged his shoulders but suddenly his face broke

into a smile. "Know something funny," he blurted. "Just a few days ago this handyman of mine put on a gray coat just like poor George used to wear and the resemblance between the two hit me like a shot. I hadn't noticed it before but you'd have thought that George was back on earth again."

Andrews' eyes lighted with the sudden realization that he had just heard something of potential significance, though at the moment he had no thought of how it could be utilized. However, he was very careful to conceal his interest.

Hours later Pinkerton received a coded wire relating what Breed had said. The detective read it thoughtfully and an idea went flashing through his mind. Though he had neither lie detectors nor crime laboratories to aid him at this time, he did have a thorough knowledge of Shakespeare and he knew *Macbeth* well. "The ghost—the ghost," he said to himself, half aloud. "Now we'll see what young Gordon's ghost can do."

In high spirits he wrote a lengthy telegram in code to Andrews, outlining in detail just how the strange similarity between his man, Green, and the murder victim, could be put to effective use in accomplishing their purpose.

In Atkinson, Andrews read his chief's instructions with no little personal chagrin for, as a seasoned detective, he had prided himself on imaginative ability, and he wondered why Pinkerton's strategy had not occurred to him immediately on hearing Breed's assertion that Green and George Gordon resembled each other. And as Andrews pondered further over Pinkerton's plan, he recalled significant facts that he had learned days before—facts which fitted perfectly into the strategy that he was instructed to follow. He had been told that Drysdale, despite his apparent placid nature, was highly nervous, emotional, and to some degree superstitious. He also had learned, though he paid no attention to such gossip at the time, that the so-called Rocky Creek area in the outskirts of the town, was often spoken of by old-timers as being "spooky," with scary shadows, and children feared to venture there after dark. Why these circumstances had not come instantly to mind after listening to Breed he did not know; he asked the question over and over with a definite feeling of injured pride. Now there was nothing to do but to ignore his hurt and follow orders, though he admitted that they were none too simple.

He spent the next several days with Drysdale at the plantation but this time he carefully planned their departure so that they would not arrive in Atkinson until after dark. With Andrews in the lead, they finally reached the outskirts of town and the detective deliberately led his mount over a path that would take them through the woods to Rocky Creek.

Drysdale sensed the move and quickly called out to his companion:

"Let's not go this way. The Rocky Creek trail is bad at night—the other one's better at this time of day."

"But this one is shorter," Andrews shouted, "and I'm late for an appointment."

Drysdale's continuing protests were lost in the noise of horses' hoofs trotting over rocky ground but the detective felt certain that he sensed the significance of the other's objections.

They had just reached Rocky Creek when a shadowy figure, silhouetted against the trees in semidarkness, darted across their path. The face was not visible to either man, nor was the clothing, but there was no mistaking the fact that it was a male form.

"Let's get out of here," Drysdale shouted, with nervousness in his voice.

"What's up—we're nearly home," Andrews remarked drily.

"I'm getting out of here in a hurry," Drysdale cried, looking anxiously about him for a detour but there was none. He spurred his horse into a gallop and was soon in the lead. When they dismounted in front of his home,

Andrews looked at him closely in the glare of a porch light and noted that his face was deathly pale and his hands were trembling. With a cheery "Good night," the detective rode away, confident that Pinkerton's strategy was sound.

The next day Mrs. Potter called on Mrs. Drysdale, who said that her husband was ill; he had returned home with a fever and was "pacing his bedroom like a crazy man."

Days later when he returned to his office, his face was haggard and his hands shook. He sent for his "friend" Andrews and suggested that they take a walk. "You have such a quieting effect on me," he confided.

In the meantime Andrews and Mrs. Potter, having coffee at the hotel, had exchanged experiences and discussed new instructions from Pinkerton. His latest plan was still more daring but his feminine aide knew better than to question.

Carefully following orders, she arranged for a riding party and after a lively canter, the group found itself passing the Drysdale home. At that precise moment Mrs. Potter screamed and tumbled from her mount. Feigning intense pain, she was picked up by Mrs. Drysdale and a servant. They carried her into the house, insisting that she stay until she had recovered. Her room adjoined Drysdale's—and Mrs. Potter now found herself exactly where she wanted to be.

While she was recovering slowly, Drysdale left with Andrews for another visit to the plantation but before their departure Green, the young operative who looked like the murdered man, had received minute instructions from Andrews and told that on his next appearance in Rocky Creek he should be considerably more daring.

On the morning following the arrival of the two men at the plantation, Andrews hid behind a spreading shrub and watched his companion's puzzling behavior as he walked slowly toward a clump of trees, as if he were counting steps. He looked furtively about and then hurried away.

Andrews again timed their return and as before it was growing dark when they approached the creek. Again Drys-

dale demurred when his companion turned on the path
leading directly to Rocky Creek but the detective was
adamant and laughed aloud at the other. "What's gotten
into you?" he called out. "We went this way last time and
nothing happened." Continuing protests were ignored.

Suddenly the same ghostlike figure appeared again but
this time the face, topped with matted, bloody hair, was
turned directly at the riders and, despite the dim light,
both men could see that the gray coat was streaked with
red.

"I'm going back—now—I'm getting away from here,"
Drysdale shrieked.

"What's wrong? We're nearly there," Andrews called
back.

"Didn't you see it—that thing—didn't you see that . . . ?"

"I didn't see a thing," the detective exclaimed. "You must
be tired out again. Come on."

"I won't; I saw too much." Drysdale made a hysterical
cry. "I saw—I saw a—ghost!"

"You're imagining things. If there was anything wouldn't
I have seen it? Pull yourself together and come on."

Drysdale could not be quieted and Andrews noted that
he was swaying on his mount. With great difficulty, the
detective finally persuaded him to continue the ride to his
home.

That night Mrs. Potter, whose "recovery" was slower than
had been expected, heard her host moaning in his room
and talking to himself, but his words were inaudible.

Pinkerton, advised of these developments, surmised that
a break was near and left Chicago to hurry back to Atkinson
well-prepared for the climax. In his suitcase was a large
bottle filled with a deep red fluid that looked like blood.
He gave it to Mrs. Potter and told her how to use it—an
order that the woman did not exactly like.

Near midnight when all was silent in the Drysdale home,
Mrs. Potter slipped out of bed, dressed and tiptoed out, the

bottle of red liquid well concealed. She hurried to the creek and returned home as quietly as she had left. In her wake was a gory trail, extending from the creek bank to the garden path and into the hall.

The next morning Mrs. Drysdale told her guest that her husband was suffering from nosebleed, and Drysdale, after discovering the "blood," was forced back to bed. He sent for Andrews to comfort him and explained that a burglar must have cut himself trying to force an entrance to the house.

A few nights later Mrs. Potter, reading late in her bedroom, was startled to see Drysdale, in night clothes and slippers, moving over the veranda. Reaching for her wrapper, she followed him as he walked with apparently unseeing eyes to the creek, waded into shallow water, and returned home. Not until later did she learn that he was a somnambulist!

Pinkerton by now was growing even more impatient and he directed young Green to appear nightly at Drysdale's home in his ghost make-up and to make himself seen as often as possible. Green, however, encountered unexpected complications. On several occasions Drysdale, moving outdoors in night clothes, stared at him in stony silence. He was again walking in his sleep. On another night Drysdale, under a similar spell, was trailed to the creek where he waded in and groped about a large stone halfway from the bank.

For a time this last behavior puzzled Pinkerton until he suddenly recalled that two of the stolen gold pieces had been found on the creek bank and he wondered whether more of the coin might be buried there. Weeks passed before he found the answer.

Drysdale, meanwhile, was being terrified almost nightly by the "apparition," as he called it, and his health was failing. Pinkerton decided to become still bolder.

Mrs. Potter, no longer able to feign illness, was preparing to return to the hotel, which meant that time for drastic measures was growing short. That night, when Drysdale was sleeping alone, she tiptoed into the bedroom. In the morning there was "blood" on his bedclothes and he collapsed.

Hours later, when he had partially recovered, he sent for Andrews, asking him for a favor. "There's a package of important papers on my desk in my private office," he said. "I'd be ever so grateful if you'd get it for me. I'm simply too sick to leave my bed."

Andrews grasped the unexpected opportunity. Once in Drysdale's inner office, he sprinkled more of the bloodlike fluid on chairs and desks, and returned to the sick man with the papers. Drysdale reached eagerly for the parcel and fainted. Its wrappings were stained with red.

Mrs. Drysdale sent for the doctor who said that her husband was badly in need of rest and ordered him to bed for several days, which fortuitously gave Pinkerton the opportunity for which he had been hoping. The next night he went with Andrews to the creek. By lantern light they waded into the water, moving a boulder at the spot where Drysdale had been on his earlier visits, and uncovered a large iron box. In it was the coin stolen from the bank.

They went later to Drysdale's plantation and dug around the trees where he had been pacing steps. Buried there was the missing currency.

Pinkerton now fully realized the difficulty of his position and the serious dilemma that he faced. Though there was no doubt of Drysdale's guilt, he still questioned whether a jury would convict on only circumstantial evidence. There was not only the danger of the detective being accused of harassing his subject into insanity but still another hazard—if Drysdale was a somnambulist he might plead that he had committed the murder in his sleep. What Pinkerton needed was a confession. He decided to play his trump card and gamble with his reputation.

With the approval of the bankers, he prepared an affidavit accusing Drysdale of the crime and presented it to the justice of the peace, requesting a warrant of arrest. The judge, dumfounded, signed the paper with some misgivings and Pinkerton took it to the sheriff who insisted that "there must be some terrible mistake." However, he had no alternative but to do his duty.

With Pinkerton he walked to the accused man's office and handed him the warrant. Drysdale took it in his hand, glanced at it for an instant, and fainted. As soon as he had been revived, he vigorously protested his innocence, insisting that the charge was absurd. "Why don't you come with us to the bank and tell them so," Pinkerton suggested—a move that he had thoughtfully contemplated in advance.

"I'll go if my good friend Andrews will accompany me," Drysdale replied. "I can count on him to stand by me."

Andrews, who was waiting in his hotel room for such a summons, responded eagerly when a messenger brought him Drysdale's request and the party soon was on its way to the bank. Scarcely had they entered than Green, in his ghost attire, appeared from behind the murdered teller's desk, his gray coat again red-stained, and his hair matted. Drysdale collapsed but when he regained his senses he pointed an accusing finger at the bankers, shouting protests and pleas of innocence.

It was then that Pinkerton confronted him with the note taken from the fireplace and told him how they had found the buried coin in the creek bed and the currency on his plantation. As he listened, Drysdale, his face ashen, squirmed in his chair and clenched his fists. Suddenly he rose to his feet and screamed hysterically: "My God, I am guilty—I've suffered tortures—I can't stand this any longer—let me get it off my mind."

Tearfully Drysdale explained that he was heavily in debt and that he had gone to the bank to borrow $1252 to pay for slaves he had just purchased. "Something just came over me when I saw George counting the money," he said falteringly. "Well, you know the rest—and now I'm really glad it's all over."

It was the story that Pinkerton had reconstructed long before when he first had pieced together the bits of evidence found in the bank.

As the sheriff moved toward the confessed murderer, Drysdale turned tearfully to Andrews. "Tell my wife to keep up her courage," he sobbed. "Tell her that at last I'm feeling better."

With that he moved toward the toilet, stepped in and closed the door. A moment later a shot was heard. Drysdale lay lifeless on the floor, a revolver in his hand. Ironically, he died under the same roof as his victim.

Allan Pinkerton's accomplishments in this case and in many others might never have been but for a seemingly unimportant incident in his early life. Had it not occurred, he might have spent his entire life making barrels rather than as a detective.

The son of a police sergeant, he had spent his boyhood in Glasgow, Scotland, leaving school to take his first job as a cooper's apprentice. He had almost mastered the craft when romance crossed his path. He was married in 1842 and a day after the ceremony he sailed with his bride, Joan, for the United States. In a way, it was a voyage to escape arrest, for the young groom had grievously antagonized the government by zealous activities for political reforms.

They settled in Chicago where Allan found work as a barrel maker for a brewery, only to leave months later with his wife for the nearby town of Dundee. There as a cooper he opened his own shop and met with quick success.

It was an ambition to increase his profits that led unexpectedly to the abrupt turn in his career. Irked by the high cost of lumber for his barrels, he decided to explore a nearby island, supposedly uninhabited, hoping that he might find the wood he needed. Rowing out to the place, he was surprised to find trails through tall grass and remnants of a camp. Suspecting that these might indicate wrongdoing, he reported his discovery to the sheriff, who accompanied him back to the island. The final result was the capture of a gang of counterfeiters and the uncovering of a large cache of spurious money.

Word of young Pinkerton's resourcefulness spread fast and a short time later when considerable counterfeit coin was being passed among small merchants, he undertook to find the lone member of the gang who had escaped arrest. He finally located the fugitive, played the role of a willing accomplice, and brought him to justice.

Allan needed only the thrill of these early experiences to realize that his life's work should turn to law enforcement rather than barrel making. His amateur achievements had become widely known and when a call came from Chicago to become a deputy sheriff, he accepted with little hesitation. He sold his shop and a new career began.

In relatively short time he was demonstrating rare ingenuity, a tenacity of purpose, and an uncanny memory for faces. The Post Office Department engaged him as a special agent—but not for long.

In 1851 he opened a detective agency of his own. He called it Pinkerton's National Detective Agency, not realizing that it would be functioning more than a century later, passing through four generations of his kin. For a trademark, he used the image of a human eye with the legend WE NEVER SLEEP. In time someone coined the words "private eye," a designation still in popular usage today.

At the outset he set strict rules of policy. He would not handle divorce cases or investigate jurors, nor would anyone in his employ ever accept a reward.

Railroads, harassed by train robbers and freight thieves, engaged his services. His staff, small at first, grew rapidly and business flourished as news of one successful manhunt after another spread about the country. Allan, of course, was the guiding genius of the enterprise, not only directing his men but often personally leading the pursuit of wanted men. His accomplishments were the more remarkable since he lacked such present-day facilities as automobiles, tele-type, and radio. Frequently he resorted to disguises and as circumstances demanded he often worked his way into the confidence of underworld characters.

At a time when jewelers were suffering heavy losses at the hands of thieves, he organized the Jewelry Security Alliance, which the agency still serves.

Eventually, Allan's two sons, William and Robert, joined their father and soon were demonstrating that they pos-sessed many of his skills in crime detection.

Several books have been written, and there could be more, relating the colorful and often sensational experiences of the Pinkertons. Of these none is more fascinating than their work over twenty-five years in finally recovering the famous Gainsborough painting, *The Duchess of Devonshire*, which was stolen in 1876 from a London art gallery. By contacting the thief himself through underworld connec-tions, they succeeded in luring him into a Pinkerton office where he agreed to return the priceless picture which he did a day later.

Today, in 1967, the Pinkerton National Detective Agency, 117 years after its founding in 1850, functions throughout the United States and Canada with a personnel of more than 19,000 men and women—and a Pinkerton, a great-grandson of the original Allan, is its president. He is Robert A. Pinkerton II, who became head of the agency in 1930 at the age of twenty-six.

William A. Pinkerton, eldest son of the founder, died in 1923, sixteen years after the demise of his younger brother, Robert A. The latter's son, Allan II, took over the reins of the business after his father's death, remaining in this capacity until 1930 when he succumbed. The presidency then passed to his eldest son, Robert, the present head.

In addition to forty-five branch offices of the Pinkerton Agency in the United States and twelve "sub-offices" in similar communities, there are five branches in Canada, besides a small army of correspondents in every part of the free world—a far dream from the fondest ambitions of Allan Pinkerton who established the firm more than a century ago with one small office and half a dozen assistants.

Chapter 2

"A Great Detective"

Raymond C. Schindler

Homer S. Cummings, who served as Attorney General of
the United States for six years under President Franklin
D. Roosevelt, once paid a significant tribute to a widely
acclaimed detective. "In my judgment," he wrote, "Raymond
C. Schindler is a great detective. He has at his fingertips
the techniques of his craft. He never falls into the error
of yielding to snap judgment and never evolves theories of
his cases until the last scrap of evidence has been developed."

To support his statement, Cummings well might have
cited almost any one of the many strange cases in which
Schindler achieved brilliant success, such as the time he
turned playwright, conceiving and actually producing a
drama with a tragic ending to trap the murderer of a little
girl, a crime for which an innocent man was awaiting trial.

Another of the detective's triumphs resulted in the conviction of a clique of bribe-taking supervisors betrayed by
a fantastic scheme in which Schindler set up a pseudo proj-
ect to tear up the famous Atlantic City boardwalk and
substitute concrete paving. Also outstanding was his work
in bringing about the acquittal of Count Alfred de Marigny
who in 1943 was arrested for the murder of his multi-
millionaire father-in-law, Sir Harry Oakes, in the Bahamas.
At the height of a sensational trial, Schindler completely
shattered the prosecution's most pivotal point by demon-

strating to a jury that a fingerprint of the defendant had been deliberately transferred from one place to another.

Like Allan Pinkerton, Schindler had stumbled into the field of crime detection by a strange prank of fate; his early years had been spent as an unsuccessful insurance agent, a typewriter salesman, and a gold miner. Unlike the pioneer detective, however, he worked with the help of modern scientific facilities—the crime laboratory, the lie detector, and present-day means of fast transportation and communication. Both men, operating years apart, were unusually resourceful, imaginative, and worked with bulldog tenacity.

Schindler, still pictured by friends and associates as a large, muscular man with soft gray hair, bushy eyebrows, and a sharply pointed nose, was a native of New York, born in 1882. His father, John, an insurance executive, had attained success the hard way and believed that boys should learn the labor equivalent of a dollar. Young Raymond began by ushering in a theater on Saturdays and later by delivering newspapers for thirty-five cents a day.

At eighteen he put his books aside and started out to make his way as an insurance agent, but his first customer proved to be his last. The man was a music store owner in Alliance, Ohio, and to gain his friendship the boy devoted most of his time trying to persuade friends to buy musical instruments. Months later the senior Schindler learned that his son's commissions totaled only $18 and he sternly voiced his disapproval. What he did not recognize was that Raymond was developing an ability to meet people, to mix with them and to share their confidence—qualities that were to prove invaluable in later years after he had turned detective.

Young Schindler moved to Pittsburgh where he sold typewriters with some success. He had saved $2400 in two years when he heard of a gold mining operation in northern California and adventure beckoned. He traveled west, invested his savings with the mining company, and went to work bossing construction of a tunnel. The job ended when his employers ran out of money. The young worker, however, had caught the gold fever.

He wandered about the Mother Lode, lost money that he had persuaded his father to invest, and finally found himself out of work when the government stopped hydraulic mining. In desperation he turned toward San Francisco, little thinking that through disaster would come the turning point in his career.

He arrived there on the morning of April 19, 1906, a day after the city had been devastated by earthquake and set afire. San Francisco was in chaos and weeks slipped by before he could even think of seeking work. Then, by chance, he picked up a newspaper and read an advertisement calling for young men to do "research work" for the Western Historical Society. Schindler applied and was hired. His assignment was to ascertain how seriously downtown buildings had been damaged by earthquake before they were consumed by fire.

He undertook the work with alacrity, not suspecting that he was actually gathering data for welching fire insurance companies eager to prove that destruction was due to "an act of God," the quake, rather than to fire, against which property owners were heavily insured. His earnestness and meticulous ways came to the attention of a well-known lawyer, Hiram W. Johnson, later to become the Republican Governor of California and finally a United States Senator.

Johnson hired the young man to probe the background of a complicated case and when the work was done, Schindler rendered a bill for $50. In return he received a check for $500 with a note in which Johnson said that it was a serious mistake for anyone to undervaluate his services.

This was at a time when San Francisco was in the hands of a corrupt administration and a group of civic leaders had launched a movement to clean up City Hall. Because a graft prosecution would require the help of a skillful investigator, President Theodore Roosevelt had been asked for help and he arranged for the services of a noted detective, William J. Burns, who had distinguished himself in the United States Secret Service.

In San Francisco, Burns soon met Hiram Johnson, an old friend, and on the latter's recommendation Schindler was engaged to organize a corps of men to unearth evidence under Burns' direction.

(Burns' work in the San Francisco graft prosecution and other celebrated cases will be detailed in another chapter of this book.)

After Schindler had completed his initial task, he formed a dummy improvement club for the announced purpose of opposing the graft prosecution which some reactionaries believed would jeopardize the city's reputation. This enabled him to ascertain who were the opponents of the prosecution and he had voluminous reports for Burns when time came for questioning of prospective jurors. He also had gathered much valuable evidence but his role was little known.

When the San Francisco cases finally had been terminated, Burns decided in 1909 to withdraw from government service and open his own detective agency, capitalizing on his nationwide publicity. Schindler readily agreed to open and manage its New York office.

Two years later he resigned to establish an organization of his own. This he headed until his death, July 1, 1959. It still operates under the management of his son, with offices in New York and Beverly Hills, California.

Schindler was successful almost from the start and his agency gradually assumed worldwide proportions with representatives throughout this country and abroad. Men in high places became his friends and they spoke enthusiastically of his accomplishments. Not content to rely on his own innate intuition as an investigator, he studied hard, mastering the latest scientific advances in crime detection. He seemed to know just how to meet any situation.

He was credited with always ignoring public opinion when undertaking a case, choosing rather to start at the beginning in his own way, learning the facts for himself, and reaching his own conclusions. While he was relentless in pursuing the guilty, he was equally concerned with vindicating those whom he believed to be wrongfully accused. He sent large bills to wealthy clients and sometimes, when a situation warranted, he worked for nothing.

Calls for his services came from many places and from widely different types of people. It was not unusual for him to leave his desk on short notice, hastening to a railroad depot or, in later years, an airport. He moved his men about as circumstances demanded and always kept in closest touch with them.

The murder case which many believe best illustrates Schindler's extraordinary skills well might have bested Sherlock Holmes. Some insist that it is unparalleled in crime detection. Its initial locale was New Jersey's popular Asbury Park, though the detective and his men were obliged to move from place to place in a rapid-fire drama before a confession could be wrung from a murderer through an ingenious and imaginative ruse.

It began early in 1911 when pretty ten-year-old Marie Smith's parents became alarmed over her failure to return home from school. After first contacting her playmates and then her teacher, they called on neighbors for help but when this failed the police were notified.

Darkness fell with no trace of the missing child. The search continued through the night and the following day until late afternoon when an officer, peering under a clump of brush not far from the girl's home, came upon her body, brutally beaten and mutilated. She had been fiendishly struck over the head, strangled with her stocking, and criminally assaulted.

There was no trace of the murder weapon, nor could the officers find footprints or any other clues. Indignation soon was running high among the townsfolk with some threatening to take the law into their own hands if the killer were found.

Police and sheriff's deputies divided into squads, one continuing the hunt for evidence; the other undertaking a house to house inquiry. Hours later someone told them of a Negro living a distance away who had been in trouble before and who, they thought, possibly might be implicated.

The man proved to be Thomas Williams and although he denied any knowledge of the crime, officers were told that he had been seen on the afternoon of the girl's disappearance walking over a path close to where the body lay. They also learned that he was carrying an ax.

Williams insisted that he could easily explain his actions but his statements were far from satisfying to those who questioned him. "I had a job to cut wood for some folks over yonder," he stated. "I started off but half the way over I stopped to drink from a bottle of whisky I had with me and I fell asleep. I guess I just drank too much."

"Where's the ax you had with you?" they pressed. Williams merely shrugged his shoulders and said he didn't know.

This was enough to convince the police that they had a worthwhile suspect and Williams, despite his protests, was taken to jail by the officers who at once prided themselves on solving the case so quickly. News of the arrest spread fast and excited people without hesitation declared Williams guilty beyond a doubt.

Fortunately for Williams, two men in Asbury Park were not so certain. One was Sheriff Clarence Hatrick who considered the case to be "too perfect" and he confided his doubts to Randolph Miller, a bank official, by whom the dead girl's father was employed.

Although Miller had never met the accused man, he was a firm believer in fair play and a bitter foe of mass hysteria. In his judgment Williams, innocent or guilty, was entitled to an intelligent and impartial investigation. He proposed that Schindler be engaged, the expenses to be divided between the banker and the sheriff. Hatrick accepted the proposal and the two men agreed that the detective's work be kept secret, for the community was convinced that the killer was in custody and no one was in a mood for further inquiry.

When Schindler arrived to undertake his task, one of his first concerns was the autopsy on the dead child's body and when he learned that this had been performed in a careless and unskilled manner, he insisted that the remains be examined by an expert of his own choice.

In an atmosphere so tense this might have imposed a difficult problem but the body already had been interred in a family plot in another state and the grave could be reopened without the knowledge of the Asbury Park authorities. The second autopsy disagreed radically with the earlier one in essential details, convincing Schindler that the first had been made by an irresponsible person. If this were so, he reasoned, police investigation probably had been conducted with equal inefficiency.

Posing as a credit company investigator, Schindler visited every neighbor of the Smith family and talked as long as possible without arousing suspicion of his purpose. Working closely but secretly with the sheriff, he inquired thoroughly into the background of every resident until all had been eliminated with one exception.

The person of whom Schindler wanted further information was a young German, Frank Heideman, who was employed in the nursery of Max Krushka, a downtown florist, and lived in his boss' home. There was no apparent flaw in Heideman's statements but since he had come from Germany only two years before, Schindler, who never took anything for granted, decided to check the man's past. He communicated with a correspondent in the German city where Heideman had lived and when he finally received a response, Schindler had his first suspect. Heideman, the report stated, had been in trouble for molesting a small child but had been dismissed with a sharp reprimand. He had left for the United States soon afterward.

In the meantime, Schindler, by resorting to another ruse, had convinced himself of Williams' innocence. He had provided the accused man with a cellmate, a young Negro, who was one of the detective's staff. After several days and nights of constant conversation, the operative came away fully satisfied that the prisoner was guiltless.

To Schindler, long experienced in such cases, it was apparent that only extraordinary strategy could determine his suspect's guilt. He found a cue in Sir Arthur Conan Doyle's fanciful story, *The Hound of the Baskervilles* which he had read many times—a story in which a dog terrorized a man to death. Krushka, the florist, kept a ferocious watchdog on his premises and Schindler reasoned that if the animal could be made to keep up a steady nightly howl, Heideman's nerves might break.

For a week one of Schindler's men hid each night outside the florist's home, subjecting the dog to a rock barrage. The dog howled almost incessantly and the lights in Heideman's room indicated that he was being kept awake but the trick failed of its purpose. Actually it left the detective with a new and unexpected problem. Because the dog was interfering with his sleep, Heideman quit his job, or at least, this was his excuse. He told friends that he was going to New York for a rest and probably would return in a few weeks.

When he departed he was trailed to Manhattan by one of Schindler's men who kept him under constant surveillance and he was later followed to a little German restaurant.

There he ate all of his meals, always sitting at the same table at about the same hours.

How to proceed from this point puzzled Schindler but at last he decided that he needed a skillful roper, the term popularly used by detectives to describe an undercover man who works his way into the confidence of another. Fortunately, he had just such an operative on his staff, a German named Neimeister, who by coincidence came from the same Rhineland area as Heideman and therefore could talk knowledgeably about the country and the people with whom both were familiar. He was instructed to cultivate Heideman's friendship as circumstances would permit but with one essential reservation.

"Under no circumstances are you to talk to him first," Schindler admonished. "That, too often, makes your man suspicious. Let him be the first to speak; from there on you can follow, and I'm sure you'll know just how to do it."

Neimeister began by frequenting Heideman's eating place. Three times a day he saw his subject always at the same table but the operative chose a place some distance away, from which he could observe the other as closely as he dared.

After several days he maneuvered himself into a vacant chair at Heideman's table but the man did not speak and Neimeister pretended to be absorbed in his own affairs. This was what the detective had expected and he was not discouraged.

Two more meals followed under the same conditions but at the third Neimeister casually took a German language newspaper from his pocket, opened it and began to read. This quickly brought about the reaction that he wanted.

"You read German?" the other asked with a show of interest.

"Why not, I come from Germany. Would you like to look at my paper?"

When the meal was over the two left the place together, conversing in friendly fashion.

Neimeister deliberately let a full day pass before they would meet again and this time they engaged in lively conversation about their former homes.

"How lucky that we met each other," Heideman remarked. "If you've got time, let's take a walk." Of course Neimeister had time—plenty of it. They strolled around New York that day and then the next until a single question caused the detective to fear that his purpose might be suspected.

"You seem to have a lot of spare time," his subject remarked on the second day. "Don't you have to work for a living?"

Neimeister shook his head and chuckled. "Not me. I'm one of the fortunate ones. My father died in the old country and left everything to me."

He had anticipated such a question and had prepared to support his answer. As the two continued their aimless wanderings, the investigator suddenly remembered that he had forgotten a necessary call at his bank and suggested that his companion accompany him. Heideman, somewhat curious, readily agreed.

The two soon were in a bank where Schindler was well acquainted and by prearrangement Neimeister was warmly greeted by an officer hurrying from his desk. After introductions, Neimeister opened his wallet and took out a check, being careful to hold it so that his companion could see that it was written in four figures.

"You want to cash this?" the banker asked. "I'll do it for you gladly and you won't have to stand in these long lines. Just wait a moment and I'll be back."

The man returned with a bundle of currency, handing it to the detective. Heideman was much impressed. There were no further questions about leisure time but Heideman did make a suggestion that fitted exactly into the other's plans.

"Why don't we room together," he proposed. "We get along so well."

Neimeister thought the matter over as if in some doubt but finally agreed that it might be a good plan. The two found a room in a lodging house but as days passed Heideman, obviously cautious, said nothing that in any way would betray him. Time and money were running out and Schindler realized that the situation called for some drastic change.

Always imaginative, he called on a producer friend who was importing crime films from France. "What I need," said Schindler, "is the worst horror picture you have on hand—the tougher the better."

The producer had exactly what the detective wanted—a revolting film about a little girl battling with a sex maniac for her life. Schindler clapped his hands and hurried away with a can of film under his arm. Before long he was conversing with another friend, the owner of a neighborhood movie theater, who, for a generous consideration, agreed to show the silent picture just once at a designated time. The rest was in the roper's hands and he was equal to the task.

A night later when Heideman and his roommate were taking their after dinner stroll, Neimeister saw to it that they reached the theater. "I'm really tired," he said, interrupting the conversation. "Let's drop in here and see the show; my feet are aching."

Unsuspecting the other's motive, Heideman approved and when the horror film flashed on the screen, Heideman's reaction was all that Schindler had anticipated. His suspect rose excitedly from his seat starting for the aisle. "I can't stand any more of this," he gasped, "and anyway I've got an awful headache. I'll see you later in the room."

When the two men met again, Heideman had regained

his composure but he explained, this time with less nervousness, that such a film was too much for him.

Schindler now realized that he was making progress and he decided to follow along the same devious lines. This time he imposed on another friend, the publisher of a German language newspaper, who obligingly—and for a consideration—printed a single copy of a "fake" edition, carrying a short item about a man named Heideman who had worked in Asbury Park at the time of the murder. It mentioned that his employer, a florist, had heard nothing from him and feared he had met with harm.

Alone with Heideman in their room, Neimeister unfolded the paper and started reading. Suddenly he handed it to his companion, pointing to the item. "Strange, isn't it," he remarked, "here's a piece about a man with the same name as yours."

Heideman looked at the item and, for a moment, appeared to be disturbed. "That's me all right," he said, trying to conceal his concern. "I worked two weeks in Asbury Park but I couldn't stay there after that horrible murder; just thinking about it upset me. Good thing they caught the murderer."

This was his first mention of Asbury Park and it trapped him in a lie, for the detective knew that he had lived there not two weeks but three years.

This greatly encouraged Schindler but he realized that he still had no direct evidence and that more strategy of the same effective nature was required. This time, in desperation, he turned playwright. Neimeister was to assume the leading role.

After Schindler and his roper had carefully rehearsed every detail of the drama, Neimeister suggested to Heideman that they take a ride into the country. It was beautiful weather and Neimeister said that he was tired of walking. They were driving over a lonely road when the detective stopped abruptly on a pretext, explaining that he suspected a flat tire. He jumped out and as he was bending over the machine, a man dressed as a tramp—one of Schindler's men—approached, asking for a ride.

Neimeister curtly ordered him out of the way and the other replied with an ugly oath. An angry row ensued and when the stranger drew a knife, the detective whipped a revolver from his pocket and fired a blank shot. With a feigned cry of pain, the "tramp" reeled and fell "lifeless" to the road.

Pretending panic, Neimeister hurried back into the car and dashed away, remorsefully telling his companion that he was terrified by his hasty action.

"Any chance of their getting me for this?" he asked over and over. Heideman tried to reassure him.

On the following day Neimeister, in his room, picked up another "faked" newspaper, produced again by Schindler's obliging friend, and appeared to be absorbed in reading. Suddenly he dropped the paper and, feigning nervousness, told his roommate to read an item about their encounter with the "tramp." It related briefly that the man was dead and that police were looking for the murderer.

Neimeister noted that Heideman appeared to be seriously concerned but he had little comment except to again assure his companion that there was no need to worry; there had been no witnesses to the "killing" and he was certain that no clues had been left behind.

By this time the banker financing the investigation was impatient; he had spent considerable money and he was unwilling to provide more. Realizing the desperate nature of the situation, Schindler decided somewhat reluctantly to confide in the authorities; perhaps now they could be convinced of the error of their judgment.

He called on the prosecutor, relating what he knew, but he received a cold reception. The district attorney still would not admit that Williams, the accused Negro, might not be the murderer; in fact, he was expecting a plea of guilty. Nothing that could be said about Heideman would change his mind.

Schindler returned to his office thoroughly convinced that the case called for quick thinking and faster action. Again he conceived a plan, realizing that if this failed little more could be done.

That afternoon he visited a steamship office, purchasing a ticket to Germany for his roper. Neimeister was instructed to pick it up.

When Neimeister returned to his room he took off his coat and hung it over a chair, carefully placing the ticket in his pocket so that half of it would be visible. Heideman, who had been away, returned a short time later and while the two were conversing, Heideman suddenly caught sight of the steamship ticket.

"What's that?" he asked, his curiosity aroused. "You're not leaving me, are you?"

"Yes, I am. I'm going back to Germany where they'll never find me for what I did."

"But why don't you take me with you?" Heideman asked, falling into the trap. "We could have good times together—and I can afford the trip."

Neimeister shook his head.

"Oh, come on," the other pleaded. "We've gotten along so well. You'll need company."

His roommate still was obdurate. "I have a very good reason for not taking you along," he said firmly.

"I can't imagine what it is."

The detective grasped his opportunity. "If you can't, I'll tell you why. You saw me kill a man. Suppose we had a falling out and you decided to squeal on me. Now do you understand why I want to go alone?"

Heideman was silent for a time before he answered.

"Listen, if you had a hold on me like I have on you, then would you take me along?"

Neimeister looked up with a surprised look on his face. "I can't imagine what you're driving at."

"I mean," said Heideman, lowering his voice, "that I'll give you a hold on me like I have on you. Then we'll be even."

Again the detective pretended not to understand and this time the other was more explicit. He drew his chair closer, looked at the door to make certain that it was tightly closed, and began to talk in a whisper. "Would it make a difference if I told you that I had killed that little girl in Asbury Park?"

Neimeister pretended great astonishment but said that he would have to think it over. As the day passed, Heideman referred frequently to the murder as if recalling it relieved his mind. He admitted that he had been overcome by sexual desires; that he killed the child and hid her body believing that he never would be suspected.

"You see," he once said with an air of confidence, "they've arrested another man; they'll never get to me."

Neimeister still insisted that for his own protection he believed it best to travel alone. "If you ever decided to tell on me," he argued, "I'd be in Germany and they'd never find me there."

The argument continued and on the following morning the detective saw to it that the subject was resumed—but this time Asbury Park officials stood in an adjoining room, listening closely through a door that had been left ajar.

Heideman again rambled on about the murder, for talk of it seemed to relieve his conscience. With no warning, the door swung open and a police detective seized the startled man. "You are under arrest," he said. "We've heard enough."

The prisoner offered no resistance but insisted that he had concocted the story in the hope that it would persuade his friend to take him to Germany.

Heideman was charged with murder and jail doors were

quickly opened for Williams, who burst into tears when told that he had been fully vindicated.

Still pleading innocence despite all of his grim admissions, Heideman engaged an attorney who boasted that in the absence of direct evidence his client would be acquitted.

The accused man pleaded not guilty, choosing to gamble with a jury. As the trial progressed, Neimeister and the police officers who had listened at the door followed each other to the stand, relating in detail the sordid confession as they had heard it.

At last the jurors retired but they were not out long. "Have you reached a verdict, gentlemen?" the judge inquired.

"Yes, your Honor," said the foreman, handing a slip of paper to the clerk. The latter scanned it, then read aloud: "We the jury, find the defendant, Frank Heideman, guilty of murder in the first degree."

At the judge's order, the convicted man rose feebly to his feet and listened with bowed head as he was sentenced to death.

A few weeks later he was in the electric chair. Schindler had scored again.

Chapter 3

Chief of the FBI

J. Edgar Hoover

Ask any one to name the most famous detective in America today and without hesitation he will answer: "J. Edgar Hoover, of course. He's the boss of the FBI."

Inquire the reason for the quick reply and he will likely say: "He captured Dillinger—isn't that enough?"

While Hoover, to be technical, did not personally bring the notorious gang leader's career to an inglorious end, he did direct a small army of his agents in a manhunt that crossed and recrossed much of the country for more than a year. In the end it became Hoover's responsibility to make a split-second decision over the telephone—to choose between taking Dillinger in a crowded movie theater at the risk of many lives or waiting until he left the place with the likelihood of a gun battle endangering not only pedestrians but his own men.

As it happened, Hoover had been advised in advance that the FBI's most wanted man had planned to see the show on that climactic night and picked men had been assigned to surround the place. For hours Hoover had anxiously walked the floor in his Washington apartment awaiting word by long-distance telephone call. It finally came: "Dillinger's inside, what are your orders? Do we take him now—or wait?"

There was no time to reason. In an instant Hoover snapped his answer and before the night was over the gangland boss was dead, shot down by G-men he had sworn to kill.

A year later when most of the Dillinger mob had met violent deaths and its surviving members were in prison, Hoover's records of the bloody reign showed a toll of twenty-two dead, eight wounded, three jail breaks and the robbery of six banks. Of the dead, three were FBI agents and eight were police officers. In addition, twenty-seven men and women had been convicted of harboring Dillinger and his gang. They included the doctor who had operated on Dillinger in a futile try to alter his fingerprints and his features.

Before relating the full Dillinger story let us meet the man who is the director of the Federal Bureau of Investigation. Since he assumed leadership in 1924 the once small force has swelled to 6400 special agents and 8000 other employees, and with a yearly budget of $161,080,000 in 1965. With that knowledge, the work of the FBI in the long hunt for Dillinger and his gangsters can better be understood in perspective.

Though today Hoover's name is a household word, less is known of his early life and personality than of the average ballplayer or prizefighter. Few are aware that the two-fisted, square-jawed FBI director once was a Sunday school teacher who many believed was headed for the ministry. And of the agency he directs there is a woeful lack of knowledge and many misconceptions as to functions, policies and, above all, the Hoover philosophy.

John Edgar Hoover's major concern is not only law enforcement. He has rounded up many gangsters of the Dillinger ilk, he has broken up spy rings, exposed Communists and solved bank robberies by the score. But besides fighting crime, he is deeply concerned with preventing it.

"Crime prevention," he has often said, "should start in the high chair—not in the electric chair." With this creed, he enthusiastically encourages boys' clubs, recreational facilities, and character building programs. He preaches respect for law and order; good citizenship is his goal. He is fervently religious and whether duty calls him to Maine or to California, he will probably be found of a Sunday morning inconspicuously sitting in a pew of a Presbyterian church, joining in praise of the Lord and in thankful devotions.

He was born in the nation's capital on New Year's Day, 1895 of Swiss descent and his religious training began at an early age. Sundays found the Hoovers worshiping together, the rest of the day to be spent reading and studying the Bible. Two of his most cherished possessions are the well-worn Scriptures handed down by his mother and the New Testament which was awarded to him by his Presbyterian Sunday school for achievements in Bible memory tests.

As a young Sunday school teacher in Washington, he was loved and respected by his pupils. He became the assistant superintendent of the junior department and often sang in choirs, sometimes on special occasions as soloist.

At Central High School he was an earnest student and in such activities as debating and athletics he showed unusual leadership. He rose to be captain in the Cadet Corps and at graduation was chosen to be class valedictorian.

Eager to continue his studies, he enrolled in George Washington University, attending night classes, for he was earning his way by working days in the Library of Congress. In 1916 he received his LL.B. degree with honors and a year later the degree of Master of Laws.

Leaving college he found a job with the Department of Justice. There during World War I his capable handling of cases involving counterespionage came to the attention of Attorney General A. Mitchell Palmer who in 1919 appointed him as a special assistant, responsible for prosecuting aliens deportable under the Sedition Act. Ten years later he was transferred to the FBI as assistant director and in 1924 Harlan F. Stone, then Attorney General, selected him to head the Bureau. It was at a time when the FBI was under severe criticism and Stone believed that Hoover could restore public confidence.

Hoover, fully cognizant of the tremendous task before him, accepted the appointment on two conditions—he must be assured of a free hand in personnel and be responsible only to the Attorney General. Stone was fully in accord.

Understanding the many weaknesses of the Bureau, Hoover at the outset planned its complete reorganization. Men would be hired only on their merits and operating standards would be raised to the highest level. Soon heads began to fall. Political appointees and incompetent favorites were told to look for other jobs and the new director combed the country for competent, conscientious men who could be depended on for hard work and efficient service. As an inducement he announced a promotion system, assuring his men that they would be judged only by performance. It was his way of putting into practice the teachings of fair play he had learned in Sunday school.

He also made it clear that neither race nor religion would influence his appointments. "How can we deny any man who measures up to our standards?" he still says. "I'm not interested in whether a man is a Jew, a Catholic, a Protestant, a Negro, or a white. What I look for is character and competence."

Developing the new caliber of personnel was not easy and it was not done overnight—but it was accomplished and is maintained to this day when an applicant must be either a law school graduate or hold a four-year accounting degree with three years of practical experience. Recruits undergo an initial training course of fourteen weeks at the FBI Academy at Quantico, Virginia, and must take refresher training periodically to be conversant with the latest procedures and techniques of their work.

Growing population and a new social order have resulted in a sharp and steady increase in the Bureau's work load, necessitating constant changes in methods and procedures to meet new requirements. Standards, however, have never varied.

At this writing, forty-three years after Hoover became the boss of FBI, serving under fourteen Attorneys General and seven Presidents, the Bureau functions through sixty-seven field offices in major cities throughout the United States and in San Juan, Puerto Rico. They are supervised by national headquarters in Washington, the brain center of the FBI, which is organized into ten divisions constantly under the trained eyes and stern direction of "The Director," as he is affectionately known.

Hoover has always maintained that all of his men, from the highest to the lowest, serve as a team and for this reason agents are rarely identified in the Bureau's press releases or case narratives for public reading. The entire team either shares the credit—or the blame.

The Bureau's jurisdiction is frequently misunderstood. Hoover is constantly trying to explain that it is essentially an investigative, fact-finding agency inquiring into violations of specified federal statutes; that it gathers evidence in cases in which the United States is or may be an interested party, and performs such other duties as are imposed by law or by presidential directive. Beyond this, it cooperates in many ways with local and state law enforcement officers, relaying to them vast amounts of information concerning crimes within their jurisdictions, as in 1965 when 195,662 individual items of criminal intelligence found their way into the proper channels.

At this writing, Hoover is developing a new information center to complement computerized systems already in operation. When fully completed it will serve as a rapid means of processing, storing, retrieving, and instantly transmitting vital police information, national in scope to any point of the country—and in a matter of seconds.

He is often asked what the Bureau does with all of the

facts and evidence that it gathers in an investigation. The answer is simple—if a possible violation of federal law under FBI jurisdiction has occurred, the evidence is sent to the proper United States Attorney or Department of Justice official to determine whether prosecution is justified—a decision that the FBI never makes. Questions concerning the agency's role in kidnapings frequently arise and they are easily cleared—unless the victim is found or released within twenty-four hours, the law presumes that he has been transported interstate and the FBI is at once involved.

One of the many misconceptions of the agency is that it functions as a national police force. It does not and never will while Hoover is at the helm, for he maintains that the same objectives can be achieved through cooperation of law enforcement agencies "without surrendering to the democratically repugnant concept of a centralized powerful police force."

Of all the services rendered by the FBI to state and local authorities, many come from its modern crime laboratory, manned by experts in practically every field of science, and from the almost inexhaustible files which, at the end of 1965, contained 176,306,791 fingerprint cards representing 76,926,-737 individuals.

If one had any doubt of the vast extent of FBI operations, he need only scan Hoover's report to Attorney General Nicholas Katzenbach reviewing services in 1965. In that year, when all-time highs in every field of work were recorded, the Bureau had located 14,000 fugitives and recovered more than 21,000 automobiles. The director also cited 12,640 convictions in FBI cases with more than $250,000,000 in fines, savings, and recoveries.

It was against this tightly knit law enforcement agency and its determined leader that John Herbert Dillinger and his outlaw gang chose to match their wits. The stakes were high—death or prison if they lost.

It is a sordid, complex story of gangster terror at its lowest level and of crime detection at its best. Bloodshed runs through its pages as courageous officers, under Hoover's direction, move step by step from city to city and state to state, pursuing almost endless clues over a constantly shifting trail. It demonstrates how Hoover and his men, as in this and other cases, combine their own tenacity and skills with the resources of a nationwide network of Bureau offices, each working closely with state and local authorities.

Dillinger already had become a national menace, the most desperate gang leader of his day, before the FBI, for jurisdictional reasons, was free to join in his pursuit. Had it been able to do so earlier, the final result no doubt would have come sooner and lives would have been spared.

The future Public Enemy No. 1 was leading a thieving band of boys at the age of nine. Today they would have been labeled juvenile delinquents; in their time they were just bad boys. However, as in most cases, circumstances and environment played their part.

His early boyhood was unhappy. Born in Indianapolis in 1903, he was only three when his mother died, leaving him to the care of a father who was both stern and over-indulgent. Neither ever seemed to understand the other. Their relationship, never friendly, worsened six years later when John Wilson Dillinger, a staunch churchman, re-married and his son grew bitterly jealous of his stepmother.

Young John's tenth birthday was still months away when he first found himself in Juvenile Court for stealing coal. Despite his arrogance in court, he was dismissed with a reprimand and his father realized, if he had not before, that his boy had become a problem child.

At sixteen he left school and went to work in a machine shop. With his father he attended church and for a time it appeared that religious teachings had made their mark.

Dillinger senior was hopeful but disappointment was soon to come.

The boy became seriously involved with girls and when they would not respond to his demands, he did not hesitate to use force. A few years later, having parted from his father, he enlisted in the Navy, only to desert a short time later. Easily apprehended, he served ten days in solitary confinement and was dishonorably discharged.

He returned to his father's home and to a relationship more strained than ever. In 1924 he married a neighbor's daughter but responsibility did not change his ways. He was arrested for stealing chickens and shortly afterward he turned to holdups.

His first victim was a grocer who had befriended him. After his arrest young Dillinger pleaded guilty having been assured of leniency. Instead he was sent to a reformatory for a term of ten to twenty years. Bitter and resentful, he entered the institution determined to escape which he did on two occasions, only to be returned with added time for punishment. Suddenly he changed into a model prisoner and a star player on the baseball team. In due time he appeared before the parole board. His plea was denied but surprisingly he countered with a request that he be transferred to the state penitentiary. There, he argued, he could learn to became a professional player. His request was granted and in his new surroundings Dillinger became a favorite in a group of hardened inmates who then were planning a mass break to be followed by a series of bank robberies.

In the spring of 1933 he was paroled. He left the prison asserting that he was through with crime, a promise that was quickly broken as one holdup followed another, with banks his principal prey.

The orgy ended, but only temporarily, on September 22, 1933, with his capture by police in Dayton, Ohio. He was taken to the county jail in Lima to await trial for the robbery of a bank in Bluffton in that state. On his person was found a chart drawn by eight of his convict friends as they were preparing for a successful escape from the Indiana State Prison only four days before his arrest. The escaping prisoners, armed with smuggled ammunition, had shot two guards and threatened others. Among the fugitives were three of Dillinger's closest inmate friends who were to join him at a later time in another round of terrorism— John Hamilton, Harry Pierpont, and Charles Makley.

Dillinger's exemplary behavior in the Lima jail gave no suspicion of impending trouble. It came unexpectedly in the early evening of October 12, less than a month after his capture, when three of the escaped convicts and a parolee walked calmly into the office of Sheriff Jess Sarber, presented themselves as officers from the Indiana State Prison, and said that they had been sent to return Dillinger there as a parole violator.

The sheriff eyed them doubtfully and asked to see credentials. In reply one of the men drew a revolver, poking it against Sarber's head. "Here's our credentials," he snapped. "Let's have Dillinger." A shot rang out and as the sheriff fell, he was beaten senseless and quickly stripped of his jail keys. As Sarber lay dying on the floor, his wife and a deputy were backed into a cell and the door was locked. Dillinger was promptly freed and fled with the others.

Only at this point was the FBI called on for help. Hoover directed that the Bureau render all possible assistance, particularly in capturing Dillinger and those who had effected his escape.

The sheriff's widow and the deputy had furnished good descriptions of the wanted men and it did not take the FBI long to identify them as Harry Pierpont, Russell Clark, Charles Makley, and Harry Copeland. But Hoover's men learned much more. They not only linked Dillinger and his liberators with Midwest bank robberies but identified them as the bandits who had robbed police departments in Auburn and Peru, Indiana, of ammunition and bulletproof vests.

At Hoover's order all of the resources of the FBI now were thrown into what became a manhunt extending through many states but more blood was to flow as the fugitives continued their wild rampage. Before the year's end Hamilton, now Dillinger's chief lieutenant, had shot and killed a Chicago detective, and a policeman, William P. O'Malley, had been mortally wounded while Dillinger and his men were robbing the First National Bank of East Chicago, Indiana.

Again the gang dispersed and G-men learned that its members had fled with their paramours to Florida for a short vacation before turning westward to renew their depredations.

The search was at its height on January 25 of the following year when Hoover's agents were sent hurrying to Tucson, Arizona. There, during a hotel blaze, firemen had recognized two guests—Clark and Makley—from photographs and had alerted the police who captured not only the two but Dillinger and Pierpont as well. Their rooms yielded a small-sized arsenal of machine guns and bulletproof vests. A sack containing $25,000, part of the loot from the East Chicago bank robbery, also was found.

Dillinger was taken to the county jail at Crown Point, Indiana, to be tried for the murder of the policeman in the East Chicago holdup while Pierpont, Makley and Clark were convicted of the murder of the Lima, Ohio, sheriff. Pierpont and Makley received death sentences but the latter, in an attempted prison break, was killed and his partner wounded. A month later Pierpont was executed. Clark was sent to prison for life.

Meanwhile, with Dillinger behind bars, Hoover breathed easier but not for long. Weeks after his capture, the gang ringleader subdued his guards and escaped after liberating Herbert Youngblood, then awaiting trial for murder. The pair stole the sheriff's car and drove to Chicago, where the machine was found abandoned. Since it had been driven across state lines, Hoover promptly filed a complaint on a federal charge and a new indictment followed.

Youngblood was located in Port Huron, Michigan, where he resisted arrest with a blaze of gunfire and Undersheriff Charles Cavanaugh was killed. Three others, Sheriff William Van Antwerp, Deputy Sheriff Howard Lohr, and a bystander were wounded.

Under Hoover's direction, G-men traced Dillinger to Chicago where he was joined by his sweetheart, Evelyn Frachette, who was to play a conspicuous role in later escapades. They moved to St. Paul and Dillinger soon aligned himself with another desperado, Homer Van Meter, whom he had met in the penitentiary, and with four others of his kind. Among them were another notorious bandit, Lester Gillis, better known as "Baby Face" Nelson, and Eddie Green, a well-known gangster. Before long they had robbed two banks, one in Sioux Falls, South Dakota, and the other in Mason City, Iowa. Their plunder totaled $52,000.

Hoover now alerted his field offices and every law enforcement agency in the country received a circular bearing Dillinger's photograph, description and his fingerprints. Hundreds of clues were followed without success until nearly three weeks later.

On the morning of March 30, 1934, the FBI received a call from the manager of the Lincoln Court Apartments in St. Paul. He reported that two of his tenants, occupying apartment 303 and registered as Mr. and Mrs. Hellman, had aroused his suspicions, since they spent most of their time indoors and when they did leave for only short intervals they used only the rear entrance. He also mentioned that they were lowering the window shades at certain hours as if signaling and had refused to admit a caretaker.

FBI agents and police detectives surrounded the place

and waited. After an uneventful night it was decided to interrogate the Hellmans. The task fell to a G-man and Police Detective Harry Cummings. Their knock was answered by a woman who took one look at them and slammed the door. Only later did they learn that she was Evelyn Frachette, Dillinger's paramour.

As soon as Hoover was advised of this development, he directed that the Hellmans must be questioned. Reinforcements were rushed to the place in fear of trouble and they had barely arrived when a strange man appeared near the Hellman rooms. He said he was a soap salesman calling on tenants.

"Let's see your samples," one of the FBI men demanded.

"They're down in my car—I'll get them," he said and started for the street with an agent trailing. As the latter reached the first-floor lobby he spied the stranger on the floor below brandishing a revolver. "You asked for it," the gunman screamed, "and now I'll give it to you." A bullet flew across the hall, narrowly missing the agent who had taken cover in an alcove. He returned the fire but the man had fled. He was Homer Van Meter, Dillinger's crony.

At the sound of the shots, the door of the Hellman apartment opened slightly and a machine gun sprayed the hallway with bullets. Crouching in a corner, the police detective who had remained with the FBI men aimed for the open door and fired. Out of the apartment came a man and woman, dashing for the street. The man was bleeding. He was John Dillinger, escaping with Evelyn Frachette. The bullet, fired by Police Detective Cummings, had hit its mark.

In the vacated apartment, FBI agents found a submachine gun, two automatic rifles, an automatic revolver, and bullet-proof vests. It was later learned that some time before the arrival of the officers, John Hamilton had left the apartment with his woman, Opal Long, and Van Meter's "moll" Patricia Cherrington.

St. Paul police joined FBI agents in searching for the fugitives. Through underworld sources they learned that Dillinger and his girl had driven to Green's hideout where a doctor bandaged the wounded gangster's leg. When this place, occupied by Green and his paramour under the names of Mr. and Mrs. Stephens, was located, it already had been abandoned but was well stocked with ammunition.

A twenty-four-hour vigil brought results after four days of anxious waiting. It was early evening when two women approached the place. "Pals of Frank Nash," one of the G-men whispered to his partner. Nash, a gangster, had been shot and killed by his own men a year before when they tried to free him from officers on his way back to Leavenworth Prison. The fracas also took the lives of three policemen and an FBI agent, Raymond J. Caffrey.

When the women explained that they had come to pick up the luggage of "Stephens" and his wife, the agents made no objection but they insisted on accompanying the two back to where Green then was living. He arrived there hours later, grabbed his bags, and hurried back to his car. Ordered to halt, he reached into his coat for a revolver but the agents fired first. Green fell and was taken to a hospital where he made a dying statement admitting that he had robbed a bank in Mason City, Iowa, accompanied by Dillinger, Hamilton, Van Meter, and others. He insisted that he did not know Dillinger's hiding place and once more the trail was lost.

Hoover already was anxious to learn where and by whom Dillinger's wound, received in the Hellman apartment gunplay, had been treated. Now, without a clue, he and his men decided to look even more intensively for a gangland surgeon.

Since the FBI keeps voluminous records of medical men given to this type of practice, they began their search in St. Paul and soon found not one but two doctors who had attended the wounded gangster. One of them identified

Dillinger and Van Meter from photographs, explaining that the latter had kept a machine gun leveled at the medic while the patient lay on the operating table.

From scant information furnished by the doctor and from other sources, the G-men traced Dillinger and his woman to Mooresville, Indiana, where they had remained closely secreted by relatives while the wounded man recovered.

The pair, however, had slipped from their pursuers. It was learned that Dillinger had driven to Leipsic, Ohio, with his half-brother, Hubert, hoping to locate relatives of his dead associate, Harry Pierpont. Their mission was unsuccessful and they had started back to Mooresville only to meet misfortune. Hubert had fallen asleep at the wheel, colliding with another car and wrecking both machines. Realizing his predicament, Dillinger had hurriedly carried his machine guns from the car, hiding in a haystack until his half-brother returned with another.

Still hunting Dillinger, the lawmen learned that Evelyn Frachette had left Mooresville for Chicago to meet a friend. There she was located and admitted having fled from the St. Paul apartment with Dillinger. Both had gone directly to the doctor's office. Pressed for word of his present whereabouts, she merely shrugged her shoulders. She was subsequently convicted of harboring a fugitive and sentenced to two years in federal prison.

Four days later the hunt for Dillinger turned suddenly to Indiana. There, shortly after midnight, two bandits, carrying machine guns, had held up and robbed the police station in the town of Warsaw, escaping with ammunition. When the embarrassed officers looked at photographs of Dillinger, they were positive that he had been one of the gunmen.

A new alarm went out at once. This time Hoover's Chicago office learned that Dillinger, Hamilton, and Patricia Cherrington had been seen at the home of Mrs. Isaac Steve,

Hamilton's sister, in Sault Ste. Marie, Michigan. Hoping that they could foil a getaway, agents hastened there by airplane but they arrived too late. The fugitives had fled, abandoning a sedan at the home of Mrs. Steve who, for harboring Dillinger, was sent to prison for four months.

After a week the trail was picked up once more, this time in Wisconsin, information having come that Dillinger, with several of his gangsters and their women, were staying at a summer resort, Little Bohemia Lodge, some fifty miles north of Rhinelander. An airplane was chartered and agents from the Chicago and St. Paul Bureau offices, following Hoover's instructions, hurried there, only to learn on their arrival that the party had arranged to leave that night. There was no time to lose.

Automobiles were at a premium, especially for a hurried fifty-mile trip over narrow roads. With difficulty the cars were hired, loaded with ammunition, and the ride began.

Nearing the resort, the agents put out their car lights, alighted and moved slowly in the darkness toward the Lodge. Then, as they turned cautiously into a narrow lane, barking dogs sounded a warning to the wanted men. It was obvious that trouble lay ahead.

The men separated, some approaching the front of the house; others posting themselves along its sides until the place was surrounded. Moments later there was a burst of fire from the Lodge's roof and a gun battle was under way. With bullets flying in all directions, an agent courageously slipped away, ran to a nearby farmhouse and called for reinforcements. As he completed his message the operator informed him of trouble at a residence a mile away.

While shooting at the Lodge was still in progress, Special Agent W. Carter Baum, with another agent and a constable, started for the nearby house. There they pulled up beside a parked car and identified themselves to its driver, unaware that this man was holding several residents at gunpoint, as they sat terrified in the machine.

The driver jumped to the ground, drew his gun and fired. Baum fell dead. The other two were gravely wounded. The gunman was "Baby Face" Nelson.

The gun battle at the Lodge meanwhile had subsided. The place was surrounded until daylight when agents ventured in, only to find that Dillinger and his companions had vanished. Evidently, they had fled through a rear door while the agents were trying to circle the building. Huddled together in an inside room were three women, who later pleaded guilty to sheltering fugitives. They said their companions had been Dillinger, Hamilton, Van Meter, Nelson, and two new members of the gang, Tommy Carroll and Pat Reilly.

Gunplay marked the next encounter with the fugitives in South St. Paul, Minnesota. There Dillinger, Van Meter, and Hamilton, caught off guard in an isolated rooming house, fired on FBI men and escaped in a running battle. Two months afterward Hamilton's body was found buried off a highway near Oswego, Illinois. He had been fatally wounded in the Little Bohemia fracas.

The trio's bold escape spurred Hoover and his men to even more intensive search throughout Minnesota and neighboring states but more than five weeks passed without a single clue. It was the middle of June when they received a call from Waterloo, Iowa, advising that Carroll and a woman were in a restaurant. Agents in the vicinity hurried there and after identifying Carroll's car, they parked behind it, awaiting his departure. At sight of the lawmen, he reached for his gun but the others fired and he fell mortally wounded, the second of the Dillinger gang to be killed within weeks. Dillinger still remained at large.

The turning point in the long, frustrating pursuit of Dillinger came a short time afterward. Hoover, whose patience had been sorely worn by Dillinger's hairbreadth escapes, received word that the wanted man was hiding in the

Chicago area and he determined that this time he must be captured, dead or alive.

A special agent in whom Hoover had great confidence, Samuel P. Cowley, was summoned to Washington and assigned the task of finding Dillinger. Warned by Hoover to protect himself at all times, he was told to follow the trail, regardless of where it led.

Weeks of fruitless plodding followed until Cowley finally learned that Dillinger was secreted in Chicago, nursing his painful fingers and face on which a doctor recently had performed plastic surgery. Now Melvin Purvis, in charge of the Chicago FBI office, joined Cowley in a city-wide search. It was still under way when they contacted one of Dillinger's women, Mrs. Anna Sage, and she proposed a bargain. Fortunately for the FBI, her own selfish interests transcended her loyalty to her friend.

Facing deportation, she offered to betray Dillinger if they would help her remain in America. Her proposal was accepted and Anna Sage kept her word.

On the afternoon of July 21, 1934, she telephoned the agents as she had promised. Dillinger, she said, planned to escort her and another woman to a moving picture theater on the following night but had not yet decided whether to attend the Marbro or the Biograph. She would have definite word the next morning.

In the interim the agents found much to do. First they secretly studied the floor plans of both theaters with special attention to entrances and exits. Surrounding areas were examined for strategic places where G-men could be posted inconspicuously. Hoover was consulted and decided to remain in his Washington apartment on the crucial night to be advised of every move and to give detailed instructions. Like a general preparing for battle, he mapped strategy, weighing every possibility and every eventuality. This time, he resolved, there would be no escape.

The final word came from Anna Sage early the next

afternoon—Dillinger would attend the Biograph; they would be there between 8 and 9 P.M. The trap was set. Exactly when and how it would be sprung depended on circumstances of the moment—and luck.

Agents were called together and well briefed, each told precisely where he would be stationed and what he was expected to do. They took their places long before the designated hour, some surrounding the theater; others posted in obscure places within easy sight of every exit. At one point, close to the theater, Cowley and Purvis stood together, their eyes firmly fixed on the entrance.

There was a long wait with every man alert for signals. Then, precisely at 8:50, Cowley nudged his companion— Dillinger, with a woman on each arm, approached the box office. A few minutes later he was on his way into the theater.

Cowley slipped quietly to a nearby telephone and called Hoover for instructions; then returned for the long vigil that lay ahead. Strategy already had been planned and signals had been arranged should it be decided to wait for Dillinger's departure.

The long, anxious vigil ended nearly two hours later. Exactly at 10:30 P.M. Dillinger walked unsuspectingly from the theater, his women companions close behind. In an instant, Purvis lit a cigar, a well-planned signal for the agents within sight.

Cautiously they moved forward as Dillinger, with the instinct of a trapped animal, glanced over his shoulder and sensed his predicament. Grabbing his revolver, he broke into a run, heading for a nearby alley. Shots blazed from the agents' guns and Dillinger reeled, falling face downward on the pavement, his automatic clutched firmly in his hand.

An ambulance rushed him to a nearby hospital but he was dead on arrival. His long career of lawlessness was over.

Ironically, the FBI received criticism as well as praise.

Some with a strange admiration for the gangster's courage believed he should not have been killed; others argued that he should have been taken alive inside the crowded theater. Majority opinion, however, lauded Hoover and his men for a masterful achievement in law enforcement.

Concluding its official narrative of the case, the FBI had this brief comment:

"Dillinger, who had been glorified by citizens having a distorted sense of values, met a fitting end and those to whom he had been an object of hero worship, upon reconsideration, found that their misplaced admiration rightfully belonged with the law enforcement officer who daily risked his life to protect them from the violence of the nation's Dillingers."

Four months later, as search for the remaining members of the gang continued, Agent Cowley, whose able work had located Dillinger in Chicago, paid with his life. His death followed an encounter with John Paul Chase and "Baby Face" Nelson on a highway near Barrington, Illinois. In an exchange of fire, Cowley, Special Agent H. E. Hollis, and Nelson were fatally wounded. Chase was apprehended later and given a life sentence.

Some time later Van Meter was killed by police while resisting arrest in St. Paul and it could be said that the war against the Dillinger gang was over at last.

Chapter 4

A Prophecy Come True

Frederick R. Cherrill

One stormy December night in the latter days of Queen Victoria's reign at the town of Dorchester near Oxford, England, a small boy was working with his father in a flour mill. Howling winds, shaking the frail structure, did not disturb them, though one fierce blast did force the lad to thrust out a soiled hand to brace himself. It was a move that shaped his life's career.

Fascinated by the sharp finger marks he had made on a dusty timber, he was staring at them in silence when his father walked to his side with a lantern, curious to know the reason for his son's sudden interest.

"Look at these, Dad," the child exclaimed. "Look at my fingerprints."

The father laughed. "Perhaps, Fred, some day you'll be working for Scotland Yard. Maybe this is a prophecy for your future."

Years later the prediction came true. Frederick R. Cherrill became the head of the Fingerprint Department of London's famous Yard where he was later to gain worldwide recognition as the greatest living expert in his field.

History and legend record his name as one of the most distinguished figures in the annals of British crime detection. During his thirty-three years in fingerprint identification, he worked closely with the most eminent detectives in Scotland Yard.

Associated with him through the years were such noted investigators as Sir Harold Scott, long-time superintendent of the London Metropolitan Police; Chief Superintendent John Capstick, Inspector Hugh Young, and Detective Superintendent Robert Fabian. Yet Frederick Cherrill, because of his peculiar aptitude in his special calling, stands out as one of the most famous, with a record for solving more murder cases than any other man of his time.

It is said that he could recognize a fingerprint as easily and readily as he could a face. He had an uncanny ability in remembering the little loops, whorls, arches, and other details that distinguish one mark from another. Frequently he would glance at a fingerprint and call out a name. He had a major part in creating the modern system of single fingerprint identification now in use throughout the world. Utilizing it, he solved hundreds of mysterious murders as well as cases of other types, frequently by discovering faint marks of fingers on tiny fragments of glass, paper, or other substances overlooked by cunning criminals in their flight.

His rare achievements won many tributes, among them the coveted MBE (Member of the Order of the British Empire) award, presented personally by King George VI in 1943. And when death overtook him on December 23, 1964, at the age of seventy-two, news of his demise was as prominently featured by newspapers throughout the United States and other western countries as it was in his own.

Destiny and his own deep interest in crime detection had paved the way for his distinguished career. It was an urge from boyhood days that overcame diverting circumstances. The exploits of Sherlock Holmes and of Saxton Blake, another fiction sleuth of the time, had fascinated him even before the night when he first observed his own prints on the dusty beam in the flour mill. He was thrilled by the experiences of these imaginary man hunters and he resolved to follow in their footsteps.

His parents, however, had other ideas. Despite the father's early prediction of a police career, the boy was sent to an art school in Oxford to learn painting and wood-carving. He did well for a time but fate was to intercede. At an early age he was taken seriously ill. Surgery and long hospitalization followed. In an adjoining hospital bed lay a former policeman who thrilled young Fred with tales of his exploits. The fascinated, eager patient often rubbed his small fingers over scrapings from a lead pencil to produce his prints and he would study them for hours. Fred Cherrill did not return to art school. Instead he spent long months of convalescence reading all that he could find about finger-prints. Reluctantly, his parents had consented to a police career.

He learned that as early as 1823, a scholar named Pur-kenje had pioneered the subject of fingerprints at Breslau University; that a century later Sir William Herschel, work-ing with Sir Francis Galton and Sir Edward Henry, had developed a method of fingerprint identification as a means of augmenting the inconclusive system of anatomical mea-surements created by the famous Alphonse Bertillon of France. It was Henry who founded the Bureau at New Scotland Yard in 1901 and his accomplishment intrigued young Cherrill. Long after his appointment to the London Metropolitan Police Force in 1914 and his assignment to constable duty at the Wandsworth Common Police Station, Cherrill continued his intensive studies of fingerprints.

As he learned more and more about distinguishing marks made by human fingers and how to apply them in police work, he often pondered the strange phenomenon of the dissimilarity in fingerprints—a mystery of Nature that prob-ably never will be explained. Yet from his intensive reading of the subject he recognized, as have all experts in the field, that no two sets of fingerprints have ever been found to completely correspond. This factor alone makes fingerprints an infallible means of identification.

In the works of Galton, for example, he was to read that

the possibility of one finger mark being identical with that of another person is less than one in 64,000,000; that the ratio actually is closer to one in a septillion.

These thoughts and the strangeness of it all were often in his mind as he walked a beat. However, six long, tedious years were to pass before his opportunity would come to work in the Fingerprint Bureau, a division of what is popularly called the CID—the Criminal Investigation Department of Scotland Yard. The latter, contrary to frequent misconception, is the headquarters of the entire Metropolitan Police Force. It is the CID which devotes itself to detective operations.

As well might have been expected, Cherrill was absorbed in his work from the start and eager to continue his studies with the benefit of practical experience. Fingerprints by then were playing a greater part in police work and were receiving increasing attention in criminal trials. He was kept busy hurrying with his equipment from the scene of one crime to another. Soon his aptitude for the work came to the attention of his superiors.

Ten years after he had entered the Bureau a vitally important procedural change was made largely through his initiative and persistent desire to improve existing methods. It marked the adoption of what has become known throughout the world as the single fingerprint system.

The cumbersome filing of ten fingerprints, time consuming when quick and reliable comparisons were necessary, was discarded and in its place there came the recording of single prints of right forefingers in one file, left thumbs in another, and so on. He is credited also with having greatly expanded the Bureau's files which now number far in excess of 2,000,-000 fingerprints, with an increase of more than 50,000 every year.

Promotions came rapidly for the young officer and when Superintendent Harry Battley retired as Bureau chief in

1938 Cherrill was named to succeed him. He continued in that capacity until his retirement in 1953.

When he assumed his important new post at the age of fifty-seven, Cherrill's hair, fast receding, already had turned white. He was a heavy, portly man, with a fleshy face and large, kindly eyes. He dressed conservatively, always wearing the dark black derby of the times.

His men liked him, respecting his ability and, above all, his thoroughness. It was said that he could find obscured fingerprints where they would have been overlooked by others. What he saw he could interpret with uncanny speed and certainty.

Time and again in his long career he was complimented by jurists for his competence on the witness stand; he had learned before that to qualify as an expert he must have a thorough knowledge of his subject and be prepared to counter the blistering efforts of defense counsel to refute or trap him. Invariably he emerged the victor and occasionally he caused an opponent to retreat chagrined and humiliated when questions boomeranged. One such incident which Cherrill always liked to recall, occurred during the trial of a burglar whose prints were identical with those found on a broken window.

While the jury was examining enlarged photographs of the marks, brought into court by Cherrill, defense counsel arose calling on the detective to explain a peculiar streak extending on the right index finger.

Turning to the defendant, the lawyer asked: "Have you such a scar?"

The prisoner shook his head and with the court's permission showed the finger to the jurors. With dubious glances, they looked at the digit and then at Cherrill. After the judge himself had remarked that he saw no scar, the defense attorney turned to the expert for an explanation.

In a voice soft but emphatic Cherrill replied:

"I testified that the scar was on the right forefinger. The defendant has shown you his left."

At the court's direction, the prisoner reluctantly exhibited his right finger and the matter was quickly dropped.

Among those familiar with Cherrill's career, few agree as to which of his many cases could be singled out as his most dramatic, his most famous. In all of them he demonstrated his rare ability with fingerprints.

Some point to his success in bringing about the conviction of the "Blackout Ripper" for the brutal murder of four women and his attempt on the lives of two others in less than a week during the grim days of World War II when a darkened London lived in fear of Hitler's night air raids.

The mad killer, striking in February 1942, had brought added terror to an already panic-stricken city. Not since the days of "Jack the Ripper" in 1888 had women been so alarmed. In each of the four murders the victims had been strangled and the fiendish mutilation of their bodies left no doubt but that a sadistic sex maniac was at large. All of the women had been robbed.

From the beginning, Cherrill was confident that fingerprints would identify the slayer and lead to his capture.

In his first attack, the madman left no prints but bruises on his victim's throat clearly indicated to Cherrill that the man was left-handed. In the three following murders Cherrill found numbers of finger marks—some on a can opener used for mutilation, others on a mirror and even more on a candlestick. All were from the left hand but to the detective's disappointment none could be matched with prints in the exhaustive files of Scotland Yard.

Then, while every available officer in the city had joined in the hunt for clues, the "Ripper" struck twice again within forty-eight hours but both women had fought successfully for their lives. This time, however, there was a tangible clue—the assailant had dropped an Air Force respirator that bore his number.

In quick time a young cadet, Gordon F. Cummins, was arrested but he denied his guilt and claimed an alibi. Only one of his two surviving victims could identify him. It was now up to Cherrill.

At headquarters Cummins offered no objection to giving his fingerprints and promptly put out his left hand. The marks were compared with those found on the can opener and the candlestick. They were identical. It was as if the accused had signed his name in the home of his victim.

Cherrill was the government's star witness when Cummins was brought to trial. In his usual methodical way he showed the jury enlarged photographs of the telltale prints, explaining in intricate detail how they matched those of the man in the prisoner's box. On June 25 of the same year Cummins mounted the gallows.

Another of Cherrill's triumphs was his solution of what has been recorded as the "pickle bottle murder," the mysterious slaying of a young woman whose nude body, wrapped in burlap sacking, was recovered late in 1943 from a river. Every possible means of identification, even her false teeth, had been removed.

Not until three months later was her identity established through a fragment of a coat found by a dog in a garbage heap. But when police called on the supposed victim's husband, Bertie Manton, a former pugilist, he insisted that his wife was still alive. To prove it, he showed the officers her letters and their postmarks verified his claim that they had been received while the body was in the water.

Dubious of the identification, the officers summoned Cherrill, who already had studied the fingerprints of the dead woman. He hastened to the Manton home and undertook a minute scrutiny of every object in every room. Nowhere could he find a single fingerprint. Apparently every dish and utensil in the kitchen, every ornament in the living room, even the pictures on the wall had been carefully cleaned of evidence.

Thoroughly exasperated, Cherrill made his way to the musty basement, scanning shelves crammed with bottles of every description that he hoped might yield a print. Examining them one by one, he saw that they also had been dusted; not a finger mark was to be found despite the use of every technical method at his command. He was almost ready to concede defeat when he reached the last jar on the last shelf—a little bottle of pickles. Obviously overlooked, it had not been cleaned and on this dusty surface Cherrill discovered a thumb mark which he soon found to correspond in every detail with that taken from the body. The question of identity was answered—and Manton, the husband, had been proved a liar.

Confronted with the evidence, he broke down and confessed that he had killed his wife.

Murders, of course, were not the only cases brought to Cherrill for solution. Many still cite his ingenuity in solving the mystery of poison pen letters that nearly created a scandal in London in 1935. The letters, in a woman's hand, were received by influential people. Some had blackmail for their purpose; others were filled with false and immoral accusations.

Suspicion finally pointed to a cultured woman who denied her guilt and willingly copied one of the letters hoping to prove that she was not the writer. Cherrill took the copy to his laboratory and discovered a thumb print that was identical with finger marks on the anonymous notes. This, he realized, was not conclusive evidence; the woman could have handled the letters without actually writing them.

Seeking more definite proof of her guilt, he enlarged her latest thumb print to heroic size and to his amazement the letters "nk" appeared in white against the dark ridges of the thumb mark.

The explanation, simple enough, was not quickly reached. After learning that the woman while writing had held an ink bottle with one hand, it was easily apparent that she had placed her thumb so tightly against its embossed label that the two letters of the word "ink" were pressed sufficiently into the finger to become apparent in the mark.

Cherrill always prided himself that convictions were not his only goal. At times he used his knowledge of fingerprints to vindicate innocent people wrongly accused. Such results gratified him as much as did convictions for he always regarded prints as a means toward justice—for everyone.

He often recalled a day in 1931 when he was summoned from his office by a court clerk in the Old Bailey and asked to go there at once. On arrival he learned the bare facts of a puzzling situation calling for his expert help.

A woman had just testified against the man she accused of assault. His lawyer, in cross-examination, had asked her if she had not been arrested four years before for stealing a ring and this she indignantly denied, declaring under oath that she had never been accused of any offense in her life.

She was asked to leave the stand and the defense attorney called a police detective to the box. "Do you know this woman who has just testified?" he was asked.

"I do," he replied unhesitatingly. "I was in court when she was tried in 1947 and I listened as she was sentenced." He cited the woman's name, an uncommon one. It was the same as that of the complaining witness.

Her former employer then was called and she also readily identified the prosecutrix in the case on trial.

At this point the presiding magistrate, Judge Gregory, called the complainant back into the box and inquired whether she would object to having her fingerprints taken. She replied that she would welcome this procedure.

It was then that Cherrill was called into court. Stepping to the witness stand, he pressed each of the unhappy woman's fingers on an inked pad and recorded her prints on a regulation form.

Then he hastened back to Scotland Yard. Soon he had

before him the marks he had just taken and those of the woman who had been arrested for theft. It took only a quick look to convince him that they were completely dissimilar, nor was there any police record of the witness. Oddly, the two women were of the same name—an unusual one—and the innocent woman had been identified by two people, one a detective, as a former thief. Only her fingerprints had saved her.

The case that won Cherrill probably more acclaim than any of his others involved the mysterious death of ninety-four-year-old Mrs. Freeman Lee who lived alone in a shabby old mansion on a large estate at Maidenhead, a popular riverside resort. He often referred to it as one of the most outstanding achievements in fingerprint detection.

It had its beginning on the morning of June 1, 1948, when a milkman named Rome pulled up at Mrs. Lee's residence, known as Wynford, to make his daily delivery. Reaching the front door he was surprised to find that two filled bottles which he had delivered on two previous days still stood where he had left them.

Rome, suspicious that something may have gone awry, was still wondering whether he should leave a third bottle when his attention was attracted to the next door neighbor, Arthur Hillsdon, a carpenter, who was working in his garden.

"Have you seen Mrs. Lee about recently?" the milkman called over, relating the circumstance of the accumulating bottles.

Hillsdon replied that while he did not recall seeing the elderly woman for several days, he did not regard this as unusual since she lived as a recluse and often remained inside her house for long periods at a time. Out of curiosity he walked over to the Lee home and peered through a front room window on the ground floor but he could see nothing to arouse suspicion. He had turned back toward his own home when the thought occurred that his aged neighbor might be ill, so he walked to her front door and looked through an opening in the letter box. Moments later he was running home to telephone for the police. What he had seen were a bunch of keys and a woman's shoe on the floor close to an old trunk. Hillsdon knew that Mrs. Lee made a practice of always keeping her keys in her possession.

Police Constable Langton was the first to reach the scene, accompanied by Kenneth R. Thomas, a solicitor and clerk of the Maidenhead Court, who had been Mrs. Lee's legal adviser during her forty years of residence in the mansion. Langton had asked Thomas to join him.

Receiving no response to their continued rapping on the front door, Thomas forced open a window and the two began a tour of the house but found no trace of the elderly Mrs. Lee. To their surprise the door of an upstairs room was locked but when they finally gained admittance there was nothing unusual to be noted.

Fearing now that the woman may have met with an accident in the spacious garden, they hurried through it but to no avail. They had returned to the house and the constable was telephoning to his station when the solicitor, moved by curiosity, began undoing the straps around the old black trunk. He lifted the lid, then stepped back in horror. Inside lay the cramped body of the missing woman!

While both men cautiously refrained from moving the remains pending the coroner's arrival, they observed that Mrs. Lee's arms were tied behind her back with a shawl and a handkerchief was fastened around her neck as a gag. Death, they surmised, had resulted from head wounds probably inflicted by the shoe that they had seen in the hall. Its mate was to be found later in the bottom of the trunk.

Other officers soon joined Constable Langton in a more thorough search of the house and the body was taken to a mortuary for a post-mortem examination by Dr. Keith Simpson, a noted pathologist. His conclusions were surprising.

Dr. Simpson reported that the woman had not died from a beating as first had been surmised but from shock, a time having elapsed between the attack and her demise. There remained the possibility that she had been bound and gagged after the assault and crammed alive into her own trunk.

News of the crime was spreading rapidly throughout the community and there was great excitement with the usual demand for prompt action by the police. Scotland Yard already had been notified and three of its most experienced investigators were rushed to Maidenhead—Detective-Superintendent W. J. Crombie, Detective-Superintendent William Chapman, and Detective-Inspector David Hislop.

Learning that a second search of the house had been fruitless, they began an inquiry into the dead woman's past and her mode of life, hoping that this might disclose a clue. They were informed that she had been married to a barrister, long deceased. The couple, friends said, had been affluent when they took up residence at the mansion almost half a century before.

A son's death in World War I had turned the mother's life from gaiety to grim seclusion. Clothes had ceased to be of interest and when she was seen about it was always in old, outmoded garments. Rarely had she ventured from her estate and on one of these rare absences she had rented her home to a London furniture firm as a storehouse for merchandise.

In later years, it was further learned, Mrs. Lee had lost her money and was receiving a monthly allowance from a charitable organization.

There was nothing more of her past to be ascertained and the detectives, inquiring into her last hours, were informed that in the early evening of May 29, three days before discovery of the body, an electrician had called to make repairs. Presumably he was the last person to see her alive, excepting her murderer.

As usual, in such a case, Cherrill was called to the place. He arrived with his equipment, ready to search for telltale fingerprints and to preserve them in hope of penetrating the mystery.

Joining the inspectors in the mansion, he followed a custom from which he rarely deviated in such situations. Instead of immediately starting out to look for prints, he stood silently in the living room, looking about, and asking himself where would be the most logical point to begin his search.

The rambling house, he had been told, comprised seventeen rooms in all—four parlors on the ground floor, seven bedrooms on the first, and four more on the second. Elsewhere were servants' quarters.

After careful consideration, Cherrill chose to begin his work in the front room on the ground floor where Mrs. Lee was accustomed to spending most of her time.

On a table near the fireplace lay the remnants of an unfinished meal—a half-full glass of stout, two soiled plates, a knife and fork and a second plate. Her bed, badly disheveled, stood to the left. There was antiquated furniture, much of it littered with ornaments and personal effects.

In all of this disarray Cherrill hoped to find some fingerprints differing from those already taken from the victim. If such were discovered, they well might be those of the murderer and he felt certain that the intruder inevitably would have left marks on at least some objects.

He began by examining the drawers of a bureau and sideboard, which had been opened, ransacked, and left half closed. Nowhere was there a single fingerprint or even a smudge. It was clearly apparent that the killer had been scrupulously careful to remove his prints from everything he touched. Equally disappointing was everything else in the room, even the little ornaments and a valise that had been rifled.

Hours later Cherrill was at the point of conceding that he had been outsmarted by the murderer. Only the bed, its coverings already pulled apart, remained to be examined and on this he put scant hope. He slowly removed one blanket and then another. Under them lay a crumpled quilt and as he tugged at it the bottom of a tiny cardboard box dropped to the floor. It was no more than two inches square. With renewed hope he pulled out his pocket lens for a careful scrutiny but could see nothing even remotely resembling a mark.

Cherrill, however, reasoned confidently that somewhere in the bedclothes he should find the box top. He removed the remaining linen and as he did his eye fell on a little strip of white paste board that evidently had been stepped on. Looking through his glass, he discerned two barely visible fragments of a fingerprint on the very narrow edge of the lid which measured barely a quarter of an inch in width. They were precisely what he wanted for his memory told him that they definitely were not those of Mrs. Lee.

With forceps he dropped the little cover into a bag and proceeded to examine each of the other rooms. It was evening when he had finished and he realized that his only clue lay in the two faint prints on the little strip of cardboard.

Returning to headquarters, he had them photographed, directing his men to search all of the voluminous files for matching prints. Then he sat down in the quiet of his office to consider his next move. First he asked himself how the killer, cautious not to leave a single finger mark behind, would have grasped the box to open it. Apparently, he had used his thumb and index finger, not realizing that even such a careful hold would leave a mark on the narrow rim of the lid.

To verify his conclusions he procured a box of similar

size and shape. Again putting himself in the place of the murderer, he undertook to remove the lid in a manner that would not leave a single print. The experiment disproved his earlier belief—the lid had been lifted with the thumb and ring finger.

With Chief Inspector Holten he delved into their well-classified files and their reward came sooner than they had anticipated. The prints were of the right ring finger of one George Russell with a long record as a burglar. Ironically, his fingerprints had betrayed him on previous occasions, one of them in 1933 when they were found on the till of a rooming house he had looted. No wonder, Cherrill thought, that Russell had been so meticulous in removing them from every part of Mrs. Lee's residence.

All of the resources of Scotland Yard now were utilized in a country-wide hunt for Russell that continued for five busy days and nights until his arrest in St. Albans where he was staying. Despite the impressive evidence of the matching fingerprints, he vigorously insisted on his innocence and it soon became apparent that to prove his guilt in court would be as great a challenge to Cherrill and his Scotland Yard associates as was the actual capture of the prisoner.

Under severe grilling he denied ever knowing Mrs. Lee or having worked for her. Pressed to account for his movements on May 28, the last day the victim had been seen alive, he stated that he had done some work in Maidenhead for another woman, later visiting several bars and finally sleeping in a barn because he was out of funds. This he repeated many times, deviating from it only once with a cryptic statement that someone in a pub had told him "something about an old woman with lots of money." He professed to have dismissed this from his mind.

With no warning, Superintendent Chapman opened his portfolio and took out a woman's scarf which had been found in Russell's possession at the time of his arrest and later identified as having belonged to Mrs. Lee. "Where did you get this?" Chapman demanded.

"I bought it from the Salvation Army in London," Russell answered, but he claimed to have forgotten the location of the place.

He was being reminded again of the fingerprints when he suddenly burst into tears and admitted that he once had called on Mrs. Lee offering to care for her garden. He followed with this statement:

"I was told she had a lot of money by another man. Did I murder this poor aged woman for something she was supposed to have, and had not? No, I did not figure in such a murder. I am not a man of such disposition. I am not prepared to risk my life, bad as my financial position may be; I am not prepared to take the can back for some one else."

No amount of grilling could induce Russell to admit his guilt and it was apparent that he would fight in court for his life. He engaged counsel and preparations for the trial went ahead.

Cherrill of course was one of the prosecution's principal witnesses. He came into the courtroom with huge enlargements of the two finger marks found on the edge of the little box and of Russell's prints taken from police files. Actually, the police had an abundance of his prints for the records showed that he had been arrested twenty-two times, mostly for burglary.

Painstakingly, the expert pointed out their similarity, declaring that they were identical beyond the slightest doubt.

His cross-examination by defense counsel, Eric Sachs, led to a most unusual exchange between lawyer and witness. Endeavoring to challenge Cherrill's expertness, Sachs handed him a chart of fingerprints copied from a textbook. The detective took one look and recognized the chart as one he had prepared for the author.

"I ask you now to look at these," said Sachs, addressing the witness.

Again Cherrill glanced at his own handiwork and answered:

"Yes, I am quite familiar with this chart; I drew it myself for the man who wrote the book."

Nothing further on the subject was said by Russell's lawyer.

The defendant took the stand in his own defense but it was soon apparent that his plea of innocence was entirely unconvincing.

Some time later the jurors retired, returning with a verdict that found Russell guilty of murder.

Judge Hallet put on the black cap and turned to the convicted man. "George Russell," he began, "after a most careful and prolonged inquiry the jury have found you guilty of an offense for which only one sentence is known in our law. It is the sentence of the court that you be hanged by the neck until dead."

Russell, showing no emotion, was led away. Shortly afterward, he paid with his life for the murder of the aged Mrs. Lee. Two little fingerprints, carelessly left on the narrow edge of a little box and discovered by Cherrill, had brought him to justice.

Chapter 5

Pandora's Box

George W. Cornish

The loud jingling of the telephone broke the silence in Inspector George W. Cornish's office in Scotland Yard, interrupting his study of a stack of recent reports. Reaching for the receiver, he soon heard the agitated voice of a constable in the Bow Street Station.

"They want you over here right away," the officer said. "A woman's body in a trunk . . . found it at Charing Cross."

It was mid-morning, Tuesday, May 10, 1927.

Cornish threw on his coat and hastened to his car. What he did not know was that lifting of the trunk lid a short time before had uncovered one of England's most celebrated murder mysteries, a case destined to be discussed even long after the death of the distinguished detective in 1933.

The old black leather-covered trunk was actually a Pandora's box filled with tragedy and trouble. In it were meagre little clues that sent a murderer to the gallows. It was the first of London's infamous trunk murders, preceding by twenty-one years the case of the ill-fated Mrs. Freeman Lee, related in the previous chapter.

For Cornish, who rose from a poor farm boy to be Superintendent of Scotland Yard, it was another challenge that he met with the same success that had marked his many cases ranging from murders to the pursuit of bandits, arsonists, and forgers. Notable among these was his solution of the baffling hammer murder of Lady White, the widow of Sir Edward White, in 1922, for which a youth was hanged; and the capture of jewel thieves who had stolen a $400,000 pearl necklace in an amazingly complicated plot of international intrigue. There were others which have also taken their place in criminal history, but the Charing Cross trunk murder still is recalled as probably Cornish's most celebrated case in his nearly forty years of service.

In contrast with the careers of many of his colleagues, his work in Scotland Yard was not the fulfillment of a childhood dream. He already had celebrated his twenty-first birthday on his parents' farm at Westbury before he decided to go to London to apply for appointment to the Metropolitan Force. It was his first visit to the big city and a week later, as he walked a beat, he found himself awed by the crowds and rushing traffic. Promotion came rapidly and in 1909, after fourteen years as a police officer, he won his first assignment to the CID. He was then a large, powerful man with what he himself described as a "bovine body."

His first eighteen years in the Yard had passed when he received the call to the Bow Street Station. There he was shown the gruesome evidence of an atrocious crime and informed of the circumstances that had brought it to light.

The trunk, of black leather with brown corners, tightly closed with three leather straps, had aroused the suspicions of the attendant in the check room of the Charing Cross Station. He had received it four days before in the early afternoon from a stranger who stated that it would be called for within hours. When four days had passed, the check room man recalled two peculiar circumstances involving the trunk. One was its unusual weight. The other was a small ball of paper picked up by a station porter. It proved to be a receipt for the trunk which its owner obviously had rolled up and tossed away, and the clerk could not understand why anyone would deliberately discard such a paper.

Two Bow Street officers had responded to a telephone

call from the attendant and after carefully examining the
trunk's battered exterior, one of them opened the straps and
raised the lid. Removing a few layers of soiled brown paper,
he was startled to uncover a woman's head. Her arms and
legs were wrapped in similar paper and it was apparent
that the remainder of the body lay beneath.

Hurriedly closing and strapping the trunk, the policemen
ordered it transported to their station. Inspector Cornish
and the department pathologist, a Dr. Weir, were sent for.
The latter asked that the trunk and its macabre contents
be taken at once to a mortuary for post-mortem examination
and Cornish accompanied the doctor to the place.

There the trunk was carefully unpacked as the inspector,
with notebook and pencil in hand, recorded each item as it
was removed. First came a pair of women's shoes, black,
size five; then a handbag containing nothing more than
four sticks of chewing gum.

In one of four brown paper bundles were the arms,
wrapped in two towels, and a pair of knickers which bore
the name of *P. Holt* in blue thread on a little tab. Another
package yielded the victim's right leg wrapped in a woman's
coat. The other leg was in a third parcel containing also a
skirt matching the jacket, and in the fourth were the head
wrapped in a soiled duster, together with the torso and
some undergarments. Cornish noted that the jumper bore
two laundry marks which he recognized at once as possibly
the most valuable clue yet disclosed.

While the remains were being assembled preparatory to
an autopsy, Cornish busied himself in a minute examination
of the trunk itself hoping for still further clues and he was
not disappointed. On the lid he observed the initials "*I.F.A.*"
while the letter "*A*" in white paint appeared on one of the
straps. A small plain card tied to one of the handles bore
the words F. AUSTIN TO ST. LENARD's in block letters. To
another handle were fastened luggage labels on which were
printed the words LONDON SOUTH WESTERN RAILWAY.

Cornish, now fully aware of the amount of work that would be involved in checking the laundry marks, the name of *Holt* and other clues, called for help. Establishing the victim's identity obviously would be his first step and he wished personally to interview the check room attendant as well as any others about the station who might have worthwhile information.

The attendant was of no help, being unable to describe the man who had left the trunk in his keeping. Nor was there anyone else who had seen this person or who knew anything about the matter.

The detective then returned to the mortuary and was told that the dead woman had been between thirty-five and forty years of age and no taller than five feet. Her hair was brown and bobbed. The autopsy surgeon surmised that although she had received a severe blow on the forehead, death doubtlessly had resulted from suffocation, the killer probably having held a tight hand over his victim's nose and mouth.

Newsmen already had recognized the sensational elements in the case and Cornish, never one to underestimate the value of the press in a problem of identification, provided them with photographs of every potential clue. He had reasoned well, for on the following morning word came from a secondhand dealer in Brixton that he recognized the trunk as one he had sold between May 2 and 4 to a good-looking man about thirty-eight years of age, of medium build, with dark hair and a light mustache.

The dealer's daughter was still more helpful, recalling that a workman employed by her father had repaired the old trunk. She remembered also the misspelled word St. Lenard's on the label and was certain that the tag found on the trunk when it came into the hands of the police was a different one. Apparently the murderer had decided to copy the old label and, in so doing, had spelled St. Leonard's incorrectly.

Meanwhile the detectives undertaking to trace the laundry marks had been successful. After checking a large number of laundries in different sections of the city, they had found a place where the numerals 447 were identified as those used on the garments and linen of a Mrs. Holt who resided in South Kensington. Significantly, this was the name marked on the knickers found with the body.

Cornish accompanied his colleagues to the home of Mrs. Holt whose daughter easily recognized the knickers as her own though she had not known that they had been taken from her bureau drawer. The undergarments, she said, probably had belonged to one of her former maids, since the color of the laundry marks, black, was used by the cleaners to separate the clothing of servants from that of their employers.

At this time Mrs. Holt had no household help but she gave the detectives the names of women whom she had employed in the last eighteen months. Her description of one cook, a Mrs. Roles, matched in essential details that of the murder victim.

Cornish then asked Mrs. Holt and her husband to accompany him to the mortuary and there they viewed the body. Mrs. Holt recognized it as that of her former cook but her husband was not certain. She said that she had not seen the other garments before.

The next step was to verify the identification of the remains or to find Mrs. Roles if she was still alive. In this Mrs. Holt was helpful for she remembered that her cook had been friendly with a former household maid, Frances Askey.

Cornish's eyes brightened as he learned these facts, realizing that he was really making progress. "Any idea where we can find this Askey girl?" he inquired anxiously.

"No," replied Mrs. Holt, "but perhaps it will help if I tell you the name of the agency that sent her to me. It

is located in Chelsea. I'll find the name in a moment in
my notebook."

Cornish moved directly to the agency where he was given
Miss Askey's address and before long he was talking to the
young woman. Her information, however, was both helpful
and confusing.

According to Miss Askey, Mrs. Roles' true name was
Bonati. Roles was a friend who on occasion had posed as
her husband to which she did not seem to object and she
sometimes took his name.

Roles was located with some difficulty. Admitting that
he had lived with the woman for a time, he felt certain
from newspaper descriptions that she was the victim. He had
not seen her for months and the police, after long questioning, were convinced that he was in no way implicated.
Roles accompanied the officers to the mortuary and positively identified the body. He gave them the address of
Bianco Bonati, the woman's long-estranged husband, who
explained that she had slipped out of his life several years
before and that he had no knowledge of her recent movements. Both men did give the police the names of several
people who had known the victim but none of them could
throw any light on the case.

False clues kept Cornish busy for the next few days,
especially one provided by Frances Askey, who had mentioned the name of a butcher of whom Mrs. Bonati had
often spoken. This appeared to be significant, for the autopsy
surgeon had reported that whoever dismembered the body
possessed a considerable knowledge of anatomy. However,
when the man was located he quickly established his innocence.

For the moment Cornish and his colleagues feared that
they were at a dead end. Inquiries at St. Leonard's had
led to one F. Austin, the name on one of the trunk labels
but this man also was able to prove that he was not involved. The investigators now were fully satisfied with the

dead woman's identification. Where next to turn was a
puzzling question. The trunk, it seemed, offered their only
hope, especially since a cab driver, Edward Sharpington,
had come forward with interesting information.

This man said that on May 6—two days after Mrs. Bonati
had been seen alive—he had been hailed near the Westminster Police Court by a man who called on the driver
to haul a black trunk to Charing Cross Station. They both
lifted the bulky case into the taxi and when Sharpington
remarked about its unusual weight, his passenger told him
that it was filled with books.

As to the precise time of the ride the driver was vague
and as Cornish regarded this as of extreme importance, he
began looking for two passengers who had left the cab only
moments before the man with the trunk appeared. With
only a description of the pair and their destination to work
on, Cornish finally located them and the time they fixed
corresponded exactly with that mentioned by the check
room clerk at the station.

Cornish already had reasoned that it was logical to assume
that the man with the trunk lived close to where he had
boarded the cab. Obviously so heavy a load could not have
been carried or dragged more than a short distance. It
was therefore decided to undertake a house to house inquiry in that part of Rochester Row and to start at the
dwelling opposite the curb where the passenger had stood.
This was a four-story structure, its ground floor occupied
by a store. Two front rooms in the second story had been
leased by one John Robinson, owner of a transfer business
carried on under the name of Edwards & Company. Fra-
ternal lodges rented the upper floor for meetings.

A store employee remembered seeing a large black trunk
standing in the doorway in the early afternoon of May 6
but he had observed no one with it. Of the other tenants
then available to the police, none had any information but
John Robinson could not be found and Cornish became

suspicious when he was told that the man had vanished on May 9, although his rent was paid through the 22nd. He had left a note stating that he would not return as he was out of funds. Some personal effects remained in his rooms.

All efforts to locate Robinson were futile. A typist whom he had employed said she had not seen him since May 4 and neighbors reported that he often visited pubs, but extensive inquiry at such places in the area were to no avail. A search of his rooms disclosed a letter sent to him by the post office stating that a telegram addressed to ROBINSON, THE GREYHOUND HOTEL, HAMMERSMITH had been returned with a notation that he was not known there.

Under these circumstances, Cornish concluded that there was little if any hope of help at this hotel but he was not one to leave any stone unturned. His visit to the place justified his perseverance for there he met Robinson's wife, an employee. She told the detective that although she and her husband were estranged, she knew his address and had arranged to meet him on the evening of May 19 in front of a restaurant known as the Elephant and Castle. Cornish said that he would accompany her to the meeting place.

Robinson, appearing there at scheduled time, had no reticence in discussing his movements. First he tried to explain his peculiar departure from his office, vaguely stating that having serious financial troubles, he had decided to abandon the business and look for a job. He had no objection to Cornish's request that they go together to headquarters. On the way he spoke freely of his former Army career and of his later business affairs. Aside from his somewhat unsatisfactory explanation of the vacant office, there appeared to be no flaw in his story. He willingly recalled his movements for days before and after the crucial May 4, admitting that he had frequently brought women to his office for drinks. However, he insisted that he never had known Mrs. Bonati and recognized the name only from newspaper accounts.

As a precaution, Cornish summoned the cab driver and the Charing Cross check room attendant but both declared they had never seen Robinson before. Other persons whom he had mentioned were questioned but in no way could Robinson's statements be contradicted.

Cornish, worried and frustrated, ordered that Robinson be trailed as a precaution and he turned to a mass of conflicting reports filtering into Scotland Yard from people who either believed they could be of assistance or simply wanted to play detective. They led him from one part of London to another and even to outside areas. Some appeared to be promising; others were vague but the officer was reluctant to overlook any shred of information that might disclose a lead.

Men who were said to "look like" the mysterious owner of the trunk were reported to be in a dozen places at the same time. Once there was a flutter of excitement when someone called headquarters to say that a trunk had been secreted in a coal shed in South London and suddenly moved under strange circumstances. Cornish hurried there, only to find that the report was a hoax. There were other messages equally disappointing and as time consuming, some from shopkeepers who had sold trunks to "suspicious looking" men; others from rooming houses where male guests had departed without notice—all of these men "closely resembling" the murderer.

At the end of twelve days of fruitless effort, Cornish realized that he was no further than he had been on the day that the victim had been identified.

The need for a fresh start was evident, so the detective turned once more to the garments found in the trunk and to the various people he had interviewed. He had nearly finished his reexamination of all of the clothing, when it suddenly occurred to him that a yellowish duster, in which the woman's head was wrapped, had received insufficient attention. Hoping that this soiled and bloodstained garment might yet yield a clue, Cornish took it to his home and scrubbed it thoroughly. To his amazement he discovered the word "*Greyhound*," still faintly visible on the duster.

With new encouragement he hastened to the hotel where he had met Mrs. Robinson and undertook to interview the entire staff—thirty-seven men and women. All of them wore similar dusters. In turn, each person looked at the long cotton coat but could not recognize it. Cornish was near despair when a young woman, the thirty-fifth employee to be interviewed, examined the duster more closely and began to speak.

"I'm quite sure that I wore this one about five weeks ago," she said. "I'm really positive."

"How can you be so certain?" the detective inquired.

"I'll tell you why. Can't you notice these streaks of yellow? Well, I tried to clean it in a basin in which I had just washed a yellow cloth. Some of the color ran and the duster, as you see, picked up considerable of the dye."

"And what did you do then?" Cornish pressed.

"I hung it up outside my window to dry—the window of the room that I share with Mrs. Robinson!"

Cornish tried hard to conceal his excitement.

Thanking the workers for their help, he left the place, summoned two of his men, and announced that he intended to subject Robinson's vacant rooms to still another search, this time far more thorough than the first.

Hours passed as they went over the apartment inch by inch, pulling up rugs, probing into upholstery, removing pictures from their frames—looking in every place where the faintest clue might be. They were near abandoning their hunt when Cornish came upon a wastepaper basket that appeared to be completely empty. Cornish turned it over and when he tapped the bottom with his hand, two tiny objects fell to the floor—a hairpin and a single match.

He looked closely at the match, then reached into his pocket for his glass. The match was bloodstained!

Taking this with him for expert laboratory study, he returned to Scotland Yard and sent an inspector for Robinson. An hour later the two were in a reception room but Cornish had planned deliberately to keep Robinson waiting so that he might have time to think.

When the man finally was taken into the detective's office, Cornish looked at him with surprise. He seemed to be agitated and his expression had completely changed. Moreover, he was now anxious to talk but he first inquired the reason for his presence.

"Robinson, I have some questions that I want to ask you," Cornish began. "They concern the statement that you made to me on the . . ."

"Let me talk in my own way," Robinson interrupted. "There are some things I want to get off my mind."

This time the detective broke in, cautioning Robinson that anything he said could be used against him and that he was entitled to have counsel present if he wished. Robinson quickly brushed aside any concern for his legal rights, insisting that now he wanted to tell the truth.

As he spoke, it quickly became apparent that he was to reveal one of the most shocking crimes in the history of the Yard. A stenographer was called to take down every word of the startling confession.

Robinson first admitted meeting Mrs. Bonati clandestinely on a street corner at four o'clock of the afternoon of May 4. After some conversation she had accompanied him to his offices in Rochester Row. There they talked for a time until the woman suddenly demanded money. "I told her I had none," he related, "but she pressed me, arguing that a businessman like me always had lots of money around. She said she wouldn't leave until I gave her money and that if I still refused she would create a scene. Then she flew into a rage and came after me and I guess I was

pretty mad, too. I pushed her back and she bent down as
if to pick something up. Just then I struck her in the face
with my right hand. It threw her backward and she struck
a chair. She rolled over and I remember that her head was
on the hearth. I assumed that she was only stunned so
I left her in the office and went to my lodgings in Camber-
well. It was about five-thirty."

Robinson went on to say that he did not return to his
office until ten o'clock the following morning. "Imagine my
surprise," he declared, "when I saw that she was still there.
And then I discovered that she was dead."

"And what did you do then?" Cornish demanded.

"Well, I was in a hopeless position. I really didn't know
what to do. I sat down to think and decided to cut up
her body into pieces and cart it away in parcels. I went
to a big stationers' shop in Victoria Street and bought
six sheets of brown paper and a ball of string. From there I
went to another shop in the same street and bought a
chef's knife. From there I went back to my office and cut
off her arms and legs. I made it all up into four parcels,
tying them up in the brown paper."

"How long did that take you?" the detective interrupted.

Robinson merely shrugged his shoulders. "I really don't
remember but I did finish the job as quickly as I could—before dinner, I'm sure."

"Go on."

"I put the three smaller parcels in the cupboard and the
torso in a corner of the room. Then I went to a public
house for a drink. After that I went home and a short
time later I met my wife."

"And then?" Cornish coaxed, noting his prisoner's sudden
hesitation.

"The next morning I went to my office and began to
think how I could best get rid of the bundles. My difficulty
was with the head and torso. I decided to get a trunk
and pack it all in. So I went to a place in Brixton where

I knew they sold secondhand things and bought a big black trunk with an oval lid. I carried it to Kensington Church where I got a bus to Rochester Row. From there I carried it into my office and I put the parcels in. Then I went into a public house for a drink and I asked a man whom I had met before if he would help me downstairs with the trunk. This he did. I went into the street and I saw two men getting out of a taxi. I hired it. The trunk was lifted in and we drove to Charing Cross Station. There I put it in the cloak room. I returned to my office and later I met my wife. Guess you'd like to know what I did with the knife. I buried it under a tree on Chapham Common."

This concluded his confession and when it was placed before him in typewritten form he signed it without objection. He was charged with murder but if Cornish believed that his work was done he was badly mistaken. First it was necessary for him to verify every detail of the confession. This he was prepared to do as routine procedure but he did not anticipate the long and arduous legal fight that lay ahead with Robinson and his counsel resorting to many legal technicalities to escape the noose. Through it all, Cornish played a major role, hurrying about to investigate developments as they arose unexpectedly. He also spent much time advising the prosecution attorney and his aides on essential details.

The trial became one of the most celebrated dramas in England's long history in criminal cases, a contest waged before crowds that packed the courtroom in the Old Bailey while long lines of curious men and women stood for days in the hallways vainly hoping for seats. It proved to be a game of wits in which the defense sought to prove that Mrs. Bonati's death had been accidental and that Robinson therefore was guilty of no more than manslaughter. This the government vigorously opposed, contending that he was a deliberate, cold-blooded murderer.

Before the courtroom struggle began, however, Cornish had verified every essential detail in Robinson's statement concerning disposition of the body. He visited the stores where the trunk, wrapping paper, the string and the knife had been purchased. Sales people, corroborating the accused man's story, were subpoenaed as witnesses.

Robinson's stenographer identified the duster as one that he had brought to the office. Pieces of stained office flooring were cut away and sent to a chemist. The man who had helped to carry the trunk to the street was located and explained his innocent role.

The knife itself became an important factor in Cornish's meticulous effort to overlook no detail. Robinson was taken to the place where he said he had buried it and the blade was recovered. A myriad of other details, some of them trivial, was checked, even to the prisoner's casual statement about a small hole in his office window.

Robinson's initial court appearance in Westminster Police Court, charged with the murder of Minnie Alice Bonati, was a routine procedure and he was held to face a jury in a higher tribunal. His actual trial opened on June 11 in the courtroom of Justice Swift and before many words had been spoken Cornish and his colleagues became aware of the prolonged legal battle that was to follow.

Even the selection of a jury was acrimonious, with frequent clashes between counsel. Some of those summoned admitted that they believed the defendant to be a hardened killer and could not give him a fair trial; others seemed irked by questions from the defense indicating that there were extenuating circumstances.

When the actual trial began, Laurence Vine, attorney for the defense, referred disparagingly to his client's "alleged confession" and questioned its admissibility in evidence. Then, quickly taking another tack, he spoke of the half hour that Robinson had been kept in an anteroom with an inspector waiting to see Cornish at Scotland Yard.

In that interval, Vine inferred, inducements had been made in return for a confession; in fact, he declared that the police had told Robinson that the woman's death was accidental. This both the inspector and Cornish vigorously denied.

Prosecutor Percival Clarke's opening statement to the jury, which Vine had interrupted, was resumed—a recital of how Cornish, working step by step, had successfully linked Robinson with the woman's murder. "In the submission of the Crown," he concluded, "the evidence clearly shows that the person who caused the death of Mrs. Bonati is this prisoner."

Bianco Bonati, who had identified his wife's body, and Edward Sharpington, the cab driver who had hauled the trunk to Charing Cross, followed each other to the stand, reiterating what they already had told the police.

The first inkling of how stubbornly the defense was prepared to press its theory of accidental death did not come until after the autopsy surgeon, a Dr. Rose, had testified that bruises on Mrs. Bonati's head had been caused by a blow before her death, though he believed that she had succumbed to suffocation.

At once defense counsel grasped this statement for his initial attack upon the murder theory. Holding up a piece of carpet from Robinson's office which had been brought into court, Vine demanded to know if the victim might not have suffocated had she fallen face-downward on this floor covering. The doctor said that this was unlikely, adding that he had been unable to ascertain whether some soft substance had been deliberately placed over the woman's mouth and nose.

Vine then suggested that death may have resulted from a slight gas leak detected in the office or from epilepsy but such conjecture was quickly brushed aside by the witness. His testimony was strongly supported by Sir Bernard Pilsbury, one of England's most noted pathologists, who said bluntly that he discredited Robinson's statement as to having hit the woman with his hand, knocking her down. "If this had occurred," the expert stated, "there would have been a skin injury. There was none." He added that the autopsy had shown no evidence of gas poisoning or of epilepsy.

Clarke, the prosecutor, again questioned the witness, inquiring to what he attributed death.

"In my opinion," Dr. Pilsbury replied unhesitatingly, "it was due to asphyxia or suffocation brought about by covering the mouth and nostrils." He called attention to a cushion taken from the office as probably having been used by Robinson.

For the defense Robinson was his own star witness. In response to counsel's questioning, he related in detail all that he had told the police, emphatically denying that he had placed anything over his victim's mouth after she had fallen. He swore that he did not know that she was unconscious or dying when he left the office but he was unable to account for the bruises on her head. Over and over he insisted that he had not struck her more than once and in answer to a question from the court he denied that he had ever told the police that "if I hadn't killed her she would have been a nuisance to me all my life."

Now the defense, thwarted in its attempt to prove that Mrs. Bonati had suffocated by lying against the carpet, came forward with a new explanation by its own pathologist, a Dr. Bronte, who suggested that with her face pressed against the tweed sleeve of her dress, she well might have suffocated. The jury seemed unimpressed.

Clarke, the prosecutor, inquired whether the witness believed that the government's medical expert had testified incorrectly. Dr. Bronte answered negatively, suggesting that "other conclusions are quite possible," but he admitted reluctantly that the cushion might have been used to suffocate the woman.

Frederick Roles, who had spent considerable time in the victim's company, was the last witness, testifying that Mrs. Bonati had a violent temper and that he once had seen her in an epileptic fit. However, on cross-examination, he admitted with some embarrassment that he did not know the difference between epilepsy and hysteria.

Opposing counsel then made their final arguments, the defense again declaring that Robinson had struck the woman only in self-defense with no intent to end her life; the prosecution contending that he was a willful killer. Clarke argued that Robinson undoubtedly feared that had the woman regained consciousness she would have complained against him to the police; that she, in fact, would have been "a nuisance to him"—a statement which the prosecutor repeated over and over. It was logical to assume, he argued, that Robinson held the pillow to her face while she was unconscious, a simple way of relieving himself of "the nuisance."

Justice Swift spent considerable time in his charge to the jury, stressing the need for determining the manner of death and the likely motive for murder. He reviewed the evidence carefully and in great detail, explaining in simple terms the difference between manslaughter and murder.

He referred to the ghastly manner in which Robinson had disposed of the body but he admonished the jury not to take this into consideration in determining whether the defendant was guilty of deliberate murder.

Robinson appeared to be the most unconcerned person in the courtroom when the jury filed out and many lingered in their seats, expecting a quick verdict. There was disappointment, however, when the jurors returned a short time later only to ask if they might take the cushion with them into their meeting room.

Again the crowd buzzed with excitement. Half an hour passed and the jurors filed in again, the cynosure of hundreds of curious eyes.

"Have you reached a verdict?" Justice Swift inquired.

"Yes," from the foreman.

"What is your verdict?"

The foreman arose. "We find the defendant guilty of willful murder."

Robinson was told to stand. "Have you anything to say," the judge inquired, "why the sentence of death should not be imposed?"

The convicted man stared blankly as the jurist fingered the black cap. "No, my Lord," he answered meekly, and sank back into his chair.

In the early morning of August 12, 1927, in Pentonville Prison, John Robinson walked calmly to the gallows. Among those who witnessed his execution was George W. Cornish.

Chapter 6

Dope Traffickers' Nemesis

George Hunter White

From his early days as a rookie investigator for the United States Bureau of Narcotics, Colonel George Hunter White demonstrated an uncanny ability as an undercover man in cracking smuggling rings and putting their leaders in prison. He had a way of worming himself into the confidence of those who directed the importing and wholesale distribution of narcotics.

It was to him that the Bureau's chief for many years, Harry J. Anslinger, turned when problems of unusual magnitude, complexity and danger arose. White was his trump card, an ace trouble-shooter whose beat was the world—a man as fearless as he was resourceful.

He wore no disguises; nature had made this unnecessary. Short and squatty, he has a large, round face and a head as smooth as a billiard ball. Now retired, he looks no more like a detective than a village preacher. Actually, he could be mistaken for a wrestler and his muscle, acquired during his boyhood days as a swimming instructor, has saved his life in many a tight situation.

His experiences in scattered parts of the world would provide plots for many a movie or television thriller. In his own opinion and that of his colleagues, his boldest and most dramatic exploit took place in Istanbul where he resorted to a daring scheme to uncover an infamous gang of

opium and heroin distributors operating on a global basis
with headquarters in the Turkish city.

The case began in the summer of 1948 when Anslinger
and his top associates were trying desperately to stem the
steady flow of narcotics, mostly heroin, into American metropolitan areas. Working through secret channels, they had
satisfied themselves that the source of supply was in Istanbul
and that the contraband, besides coming to America, was
being sent in wholesale quantities to various parts of the
Middle East and to large European cities. Beyond that,
they could uncover no specific details; the identity of
the syndicate and its ringleaders remained a mystery.

Anslinger finally sent for White, his ace investigator, and
laid the facts before him. "I want you to go to Istanbul
and break up this gang," he said. "How to do it is up
to you but, remember, look after yourself. I fully realize
that it will be a dangerous job—but it must be done."

"When do you want me to start?" White inquired.

"As fast as you can pack a suitcase."

White understood exactly what such an order meant. He
recognized its difficulties and its dangers. And he realized
that he must work with native police, for as an American
he had no authority to make arrests on foreign soil. Would
the Turkish police resent his presence? He wondered.

Forty-eight hours later he was on a plane bound for
Turkey. Under his coat he carried a revolver and his
wallet bulged with American currency—the necessary bait
for a fishing expedition such as this.

Arriving in Istanbul with a single bag, he took a cab
to a moderately priced hotel and registered under an assumed name. Then, waiting until evening, he donned a
suit of garish sports clothes that gave him the appearance
of a wealthy tourist and started for the waterfront skirting
the Bosporus on what he hoped would be a successful
shopping tour.

He was aware of a serious handicap—he could not speak

the Turkish tongue. However, he knew that luckily the word heroin is the same in every language, though its pronunciation varies in different countries. And heroin was the object of his shopping.

Elbowing his way through crowded streets, he looked in at the shabby bars, asking himself where to start since all of them appeared to be alike.

White entered one, seated himself at the bar, and ordered cognac. He casually engaged the bartender in conversation and after a time whispered the single word "heroin." His only answer was a shrug of the shoulders from the man who was serving drinks.

He tried the next bar and another with no success. At the fourth he withheld his question until after he had paid for his drinks with a good-sized bill within sight of those around him. "Sell heroin here—go to jail," the bartender snapped and walked away.

For two nights he roamed about but made no headway. On the third day he found a sailor who spoke some English and invited him to drink. After they had talked together for a time, White leaned across the table and whispered: "Heroin—you know where I can buy it?"

The man looked furtively about before he spoke: "Yes, down the street—a bar with a funny sign. It says: 'Fun for sailors here.'"

Nodding his thanks, White left the place and started for the bar his companion had mentioned. He found it without difficulty and it looked like the dirtiest dive on the entire waterfront.

White shifted his holster to avoid a bulging of his coat and walked in with the air of a tourist bent on sightseeing. Calling for brandy, he again took out his roll of money and made certain that it was seen. After several drinks, he caught the eye of a young, dark-haired bar girl and motioned her to a rear table. She told him that she could speak a little English.

"You rich American?" she asked. "You call me Melina."

"Call me George," said her new companion. "How about a drink?"

The girl nodded and one drink soon followed another, with White paying for each service which gave him repeated opportunity to display his money.

"Melina have nice bedroom," the girl informed him somewhat later. "Maybe you come with me and see."

White frowned. "I don't waste time with dames," he said. "I'm here on important business."

"What's important?" she asked with injured pride. "I give you very good time."

"I'll tell you what's important," White said to her. "But can't we talk some place where it's quiet. This racket is terrible."

Melina led the way through the smoky bar into a back room. "Now tell me what's important," she coaxed, snuggling close to him. "I know only one thing important—you know . . ."

White leaned across the table. "Heroin," he whispered. "That's what's important in my life. Got some?"

"No, no," the girl replied, looking surprised. "Heroin against law here."

White took her hand and his face indicated his disbelief. "Don't give me that line, Melina. I'm in this town to buy the stuff and I need a lot of it. They tell me here is the place to get it."

"What you do with it?"

"Sell it, of course. My company has many customers in America and we pay well."

"And maybe you give Melina little money for only me?" she inquired, her eyes lighting.

White dug his hand into his pocket and handed her a $20 bill. Bowing graciously, she rose from her chair and started for the bar. She returned in a few moments followed by a tall, heavily built Turk who stared at the American with a malevolent look in his eyes. He was not the type with whom White had hoped to negotiate.

"He take you to right place," the girl said slyly. "Vasil not speak English."

Responding to a nod from the Turk, the detective followed him out and along several smelly waterfront blocks until the stranger turned into another bar. White made a mental note of the street number and of the name on the door—Gazul Adana. He soon found himself in a dingy room where the two were joined by a stout, elderly woman, who announced that she would be their interpreter.

Vasil spoke to her in his own tongue and from his tone it appeared that he was angry. "He doesn't trust you," the woman said. "He demands to know who you are and what you want."

White came quickly to the point, explaining that he represented a large and wealthy syndicate in New York with connections in many American cities. They were tired of picking up small quantities of heroin in many places and wanted an unlimited supply. This, he emphasized, was the sole purpose of his trip and he added that he was well supplied with money.

"How will you get the stuff to America—it doesn't walk," Vasil remarked sarcastically through the interpreter, and the detective laughingly told him that seamen aboard a large English steamer were on his payroll.

Vasil talked on but he was still distrustful. He doubted White's ability to pay for large purchases and he wanted to know just how a stranger in Istanbul had chanced to meet Melina.

White again boasted of his wealth, at the same time trying to impress his listeners with his thorough knowledge of the traffic, prices, and the ways of smugglers. He explained how he had been told to look for the bar with the inviting sign and simply had followed the advice of a buyer.

"When I travel in foreign countries I leave my money

in the hotel safe," he added, "but I do have this with me," and he displayed his bulky roll of currency.

The Turk stared with hungry eyes; then he spoke again to the woman in the language that the detective could not understand, excepting for the single word—heroin, which was repeated several times.

"He talks too much," the woman said, addressing White. "He wants you to meet him here at noon tomorrow. I think he wants for you to meet the big boss."

White assured her that he would be there, walked out and returned to his room, wondering whether he was really making progress or perhaps was being played for a fool. In either case, he knew that in the meantime there were important things for him to do. He took up the telephone and called a number. An hour later he walked to the street, signaled a cab driver and handed him an address on a slip of paper.

As the machine wound its way over narrow, unfamiliar streets, its passenger peered intently through the rear window, wondering if he was being followed. When the cab finally came to a stop, White jumped out, paid his fare, and looked furtively about before climbing the outside steps of a pretentious-looking building.

The man who greeted him was the chief of the Turkish police, Namuk Karayel, a tall, powerful man, who had been advised of the American's mission and asked to cooperate, since only his men would be empowered to make arrests. Several high officers were present and after introductions White reported what had transpired, informing them of his appointment for the following day.

"Do you know the name of the man you're meeting?" the Chief inquired.

"I have only one name—Vasil—and I can tell you what he looks like."

Chief Karayel gave his men a curious look. "We've been watching him for quite a while," he said. "He's a slippery one but you can count on us to help and, of course, we'll do our best to keep you covered. His gang is unpredictable."

White needed such assurance, for he did not know to where his rendezvous would lead or who in the Turkish underworld he would meet. In this uncertainty, it was impossible to plan definite strategy but the Chief promised to post plainclothesmen in two cabs close to the bar at the time of the meeting, each machine to be parked facing an opposite direction so that White and Vasil could be trailed regardless of which way they went.

Promptly at noon of the following day White entered the dive and found the tall Turk awaiting him. At his side stood a young countryman, slim and flashily dressed. The detective took a sharp dislike for him at first sight. In perfect English this man introduced himself as Iradodos Terapyance though he asked that he be addressed as Bob.

The two Turks led the way to the back room where Vasil and White had talked the day before but this time Bob assumed the role of spokesman and his manner was far from pleasing. He said bluntly that Vasil was still distrustful; he still wanted assurances that the American was "right" and that he had sufficient funds to close a deal of the size he had proposed.

White, who could be tough when occasion demanded, told the younger man that his money was in the hotel safe where it belonged and that he had no intention of paying it until he had been permitted to take samples of the "stuff" to his hotel room for tests. "I was tricked once years ago," he said, "but since then I've learned my way around. Tell Vasil those are my terms; if he doesn't like them there are others."

A long conversation in Turkish followed but the American could not tell its drift, nor could he foretell the outcome. It was apparent that Vasil was greatly displeased.

After a time Bob arose and signaled to White to follow.

"We're going now to see the big boss," he announced. "At last Vasil seems to be satisfied."

As the three moved down the street, White glanced at one of the cabs and saw that it was following but his assurance ended after they had gone a few blocks farther. To his deep concern, his companions unexpectedly led him into a park and White, stopping on the pretext of lighting a cigarette, looked behind him and saw the protecting cab stalled at the street's end a considerable distance away. Now he was at the mercy of his companions and he rejoined them with apprehension.

They walked in silence over narrow graveled paths that skirted beds of blooming flowers until Vasil stopped to greet a stout, swarthy-faced man of middle age who apparently had been told to meet them there. The stranger eyed White suspiciously before he put out his hand. "I'm Josef Kariyo," he said. Then, lowering his voice, he asked bluntly: "Just how much heroin do you want to buy?"

"As much as you will sell," White told him. "My crowd runs a big business; we have no time to fool around with little stuff."

Kariyo seemed much impressed but there was more conversation before they could agree on a price. Now White's three companions led him over a path that wound its way to the opposite side of the park. The American looked again at the cab still parked where they had entered but he knew that he dared not try to signal. There was no alternative but to accompany the Turks without protection regardless of the risk. Suddenly, a new fear gripped him. Kariyo had spoken of having lived in America; perhaps he had recognized White from newspaper photographs and planned a trap. However, there could be no retreat.

Leaving the park, Kariyo hailed a cab and spoke in Turkish to the driver. As the four rode over twisting streets, White looked out hopefully for signs that might be useful later in tracing their route or identifying their final destination. There was nothing that he could read and the houses looked very much alike.

The ride ended in front of a cottage and the passengers alighted. "Here's where you'll get the stuff," Kariyo whispered, "or at least a sample of it if you're still so fussy."

Again the detective realized the danger of his position and the chance that his mission might end in failure. "How will I ever tell the police where this house is?" he asked himself. "It has no number and there's no street sign. Without police help I'm powerless—these Turks against me alone."

It was a moment for fast thinking. As the four walked up the outside stairs, White's eyes fell on a gas meter. He stopped, fumbled for a cigarette and asked one of his companions for a match. But his gaze was fixed on a number of six digits stamped on the meter and he resolved to impress it indelibly in his mind. It was his only hope.

He soon rejoined the others and walked into a poorly furnished living room. At Kariyo's call, two strange men emerged from an outer room, listened to his orders, and hurried out. Moments later they returned carrying two large paper sacks which they deposited at Kariyo's feet. Opening them, he called to White to view their contents—heroin.

Without a word the detective took a small envelope from his pocket. Into it he dropped a sample from each bag, explaining that he would test it in his hotel room. "Give me this address and I'll meet you here tomorrow," he asked shrewdly. "If this is as good as it looks, I'll pay you then."

Kariyo, obviously reading the other's mind, shook his head and muttered an emphatic "no." "We'll meet you in the bar and drive you here," he said coldly. "Is three o'clock tomorrow right?"

Concealing his disappointment, White agreed and started with the others for the street. This time he deliberately paused to tie a shoelace within sight of the gas meter for another look at its number.

The party returned by cab to the waterfront bar where they parted after agreeing again on the meeting time for the following afternoon. White looked at his wrist watch, then quickly reminded himself of the many things to be done in a relatively short time. His first move was to test his narcotics samples in the privacy of his hotel room. Satisfied that the heroin was of high grade, he took a cab to the American consulate where he would meet the Turkish police chief to plan for the work ahead.

As he recounted to himself the events of the morning, he became still more convinced that the narcotics sellers were determined that he should not know the location of the cottage where the transaction would be closed. Under these circumstances, he wondered how it could be possible to obtain police reinforcements to arrest the men, for obviously he could not do it alone.

Some time later he confided his problem to the police chief, after giving him the numbers taken from the gas meter. The Chief, losing no time, telephoned to the gas company, gave the numbers to an official, and soon was told the address of the house. White, however, was not fully reassured. He pointed out that in the dim light he may have misread the digits; in that case, the police might be stationed at the wrong place at the time of the crucial meeting.

"Always good to be careful," said the Chief. "Stand by. The address can be easily checked."

Again he took up the telephone and in a short time a gas company truck rolled up to the curb. "They'll drive you by the place," said Chief Karayel. "You can easily tell whether it's the one you were in."

White concealed himself in the rear of the truck and was driven away. When the machine slowed down after a ride of considerable distance, he looked out and recognized the cottage.

He was soon back with the Chief but they had barely begun to discuss procedures when Karayel received an emergency call that would take him to a suburb. The two agreed to meet there at one o'clock the following day. They would have about two hours for careful planning before White's meeting with the Turks.

Their strategy, as they mapped it on the next afternoon, was based on guess work, for they were obliged to assume that White's big purchase would be made in the cottage as the Turks had indicated. If this occurred, there would be adequate police protection; how and where they would be posted was Chief Karayel's problem. However, both men realized that the others might change their plans without a word of notice. It was a gamble that the detective was forced to take—but he had faced such risks before.

Plans called for White to receive the contraband and pay for it. Then, on a pretext, he would raise a window shade—the signal for the police to hurry in.

The two men were still discussing eventualities when there came an unexpected interruption. The front door of the office had suddenly opened admitting a tall, dark-complexioned man. White looked at him in stark amazement, then hurried into an inner office, beckoning to Karayel to follow.

"That's Vasil," White whispered. "One of the gang I'm working with. They must have tailed me after all. I'm afraid the . . ."

"Let me handle this," Karayel interrupted, and he returned to the outer office.

Vasil, it soon appeared, was as startled as the detective. He explained that he had come to obtain a visa for a friend but the police officer chose to take no chances. He assured White that he could detain his visitor for a sufficient time with questions and formal papers. This, however, would settle only half of White's problems.

Knowing that he was to meet Vasil with the others in the bar, he wondered how they would act in that man's absence. Would they be suspicious and refuse to close the deal? Would they, perhaps, insist on a delay? Only time would tell. White now had no alternative but to proceed as if he knew nothing of Vasil's whereabouts.

At the designated hour he walked into the bar, his wallet bulging with enough currency to close a deal in at least five figures. He was greeted coldly by the Turk named Bob and by Kariyo who he had met in the park. They told him that they were waiting for Vasil and could not understand why he had not arrived.

White shrugged his shoulders, called to the bartender, and ordered drinks for himself and the others who were visibly worried by Vasil's absence. "He's never been late before," Bob remarked. "Something serious must have happened."

The detective pretended to make little of the comment and ordered more drinks, seriously concerned that the police chief might have difficulty in detaining the absent man. When nearly an hour had elapsed, White rose from his chair, looked at his watch, and banged his fist on the table. "This isn't the way we do business in America," he exclaimed with feigned anger. "I can't wait any longer. We can finish our business together—without Vasil."

There was a lengthy exchange of words between the two men in the language that White could not understand. At length, Bob started for the telephone, his companion explaining that they would make one last effort to locate Vasil.

He was back ten minutes later, shaking his head. Again White demanded that they proceed and this time they agreed. The two led the way to a cab and as it sped away at a rapid pace White looked intently through the window, hoping to recognize some place that they had passed on the day before. He could see none but his anxieties suddenly subsided when the taxi came to a stop and White not only recognized the house but observed what was being done for his protection.

Close to the cottage fully a dozen men in laborers' clothes were working with pick and shovel, apparently digging up the street. White eyed them quickly and recognized several as policemen he had seen in Chief Karayel's office. At last he knew for a certainty that he could count on the promised help and he laughed to himself at the ingenious way that it was being done.

Without even taking notice of the workmen, White's companions started for the house while he followed a few steps behind. Once inside he looked about, fearful that perhaps Vasil might be there but he soon found that there was no cause for worry.

Bob and Kariyo clapped their hands and spoke loudly in Turkish, presumably giving orders. A door opened and in walked the two Turks whom White had seen before. In their hands were heavy bags of heroin.

White first examined the stuff closely, then took out his roll of bills, counted close to $15,000, and handed it to Bob and his associate. Both men quickly squatted on the floor and began to count.

At that instant, White felt cautiously for his holster and backed slowly toward a window. Without a word he drew his revolver and leveled it at the men still poring over currency.

"Up with your hands," he commanded. "I represent the Bureau of Narcotics in America."

The startled men obeyed and as White shifted the gun into his left hand, he grabbed the window shade in his right—raising it would be the signal for the police to come. But the shade was stuck!

Thinking fast, he picked up a chair and sent it smashing

through the window. Then he waited for minutes that seemed like hours. The police evidently had not heard the crash with the noise that they were making.

He reached fast for a second chair but in that instant Kariyo, grasping the situation, took a forward step. "One more step and you'll be dead," White cried out.

The second chair flew through the shattered window and moments later White heard the pounding of footsteps on the stairs.

Police, with the Chief in the lead, came rushing into the room. The four men were handcuffed and the bags of heroin, together with the currency, were seized as evidence.

Chief Karayel took command of the situation and from his tone White knew the kind of questions that were being asked. The grilling went on for hours and when one of the Chief's men took out paper and pen, the American detective realized that a confession was under way.

When it was over and statements had been signed, the four men were led away and White started with the Chief for an eating place. "Did you get all you wanted?" White inquired anxiously.

"All I wanted and a great deal more," he answered, smiling. "At eleven tonight you and I have a date on the other side of the Bosporus."

"What's doing across the Bosporus?"

"That's where they get their heroin—they and a lot of others. Will you come?"

White did not need coaxing. Crossing the water with a squad of men, the two led a raid on an enormous plant operating day and night to process heroin for the illicit trade of traffickers. Its entire force from boss to laborers was taken into custody and narcotics worth hundreds of thousands of dollars were confiscated.

The prisoners, in turn, revealed the location of two rival plants, one of them even larger, operated by competitors.

They too were raided and more fortunes in contraband came into possession of the authorities.

Satisfied that the Turkish source of heroin flowing into American markets had been crushed, White thanked Chief Karayel and bought an airplane ticket for home.

Anslinger greeted him with a pat on the back and a new assignment equally difficult and dangerous. It was followed by many others—but there was one happy interruption.

It occurred on a warm October afternoon in 1949 when White was called to the office of the Bureau of Narcotics in Washington and presented with the coveted Treasury medal for exceptional service. With it was a citation recalling in glowing terms a list of his successful operations. The parchment bore these concluding words:

"All of these investigations were of major importance. In addition to their value in prosecuting major figures in international rings and syndicates, they also effectively demonstrated to law enforcement officers that a serious international smuggling problem existed and that it could be solved by international cooperation in police work."

White's urge to actively engage in law enforcement began at an early age and was stimulated as he grew to manhood. From Los Angeles, his birthplace, the family had moved to nearby Alhambra, California, where his father was elected mayor on a reform platform pledged to restore honest government. The boy's enthusiasm over a successful campaign against corruption remained with him through his formative years while he attended Oregon State College and later served the Red Cross as a first-aid instructor.

Then he turned to newspaper work, becoming a police reporter, first in San Francisco and afterward in Los Angeles. In close contact with those who warred on crime, he was fascinated by their performances but he finally realized that his interest lay in pursuing criminals rather than writing about their capture.

He took an examination for a place in the federal Narcotics Bureau and passed. It marked the beginning of his career as a "dopebuster" that was interrupted only three times—once in World War II to serve the Office of Strategic Services, returning with the rank of colonel; again to work with the Kefauver Committee in its nationwide investigation of crime; and a third time when he took leave to gather evidence that banished the notorious racketeer, Charles "Lucky" Luciano, from the country.

Only months after his appointment, White's first important assignment took him to Seattle, Washington, with orders to trace the source of narcotics which suddenly had begun to pour into west coast cities at an alarming rate. He began by arresting an insignificant crippled peddler, after finding a few grains of morphine hidden in the rubber tip of the man's crutch. Demanding to know the source of the contraband, White was told the name of a Chinese, a well-known member of the Hip Sing Tong. This man, in turn, disclosed a higher-up, an influential Chinese in Butte, Montana.

The trail finally led to New York where White, posing as the buyer for a wealthy smuggling syndicate, learned that an inner group in the powerful tong was carrying on a nationwide traffic in narcotics, receiving orders by mail and delivering them by railway express. So well did the undercover man play his role that despite racial differences, he was initiated into the tong in impressive Oriental ceremonies. With this added prestige he rounded up not only the leaders of the clique but more than fifty of its agents in a number of large American cities.

Equally impressive was White's work in France less than a year later after a small quantity of heroin had been found hidden aboard the steamer *St. Tropez* on its arrival in New York. A seaman had disclosed that the contraband came from Marseilles where a man he could name only as Dominique was the principal wholesaler. Perhaps the sailor knew more but this was all that he would tell. The rest was up to White and France became his destination.

Arriving in Marseilles, he first made the rounds of cheap bars frequented by sailors, hoping that by some rare good fortune he might pick up a clue to the mysterious Dominique of whom he had only the barest description. From the start he realized that this would be a "needle in a haystack" hunt and his fears were soon substantiated. He spent days and nights in waterfront dives where inquiries about "a man named Dominique" were met only by shrugged shoulders and puzzled looks. He talked with many strange characters but time passed without result. Often, at times and places that seemed appropriate, he inquired where a bit of heroin or some like drug, might be obtained but it was obvious that if any of those with whom he spoke had any information, they were unwilling to disclose it.

Discouraged but far from admitting failure, White continued doggedly at his work until days later a nondescript drinker suggested that he try again in a certain bar operated by a man and wife—two people of whom the investigator had not heard.

White soon was buying drinks for the couple and before long he displayed a roll of bills, explaining that he was in France to augment the supply of narcotics for his wealthy American associates. After he had made small purchases from the couple, they told him that he should meet a man named Dominique and arranged a midnight contact in a dark and deserted alley. Dominique first accepted currency for a large purchase; then, growing suspicious, he turned on the American with a stiletto but White quickly overpowered him. With handcuffs on his wrists, Dominique was turned over to French police and his associates in a powerful smuggling ring soon were brought to justice.

Other successful experiences followed in Ecuador and in neighboring southern countries. In Houston, Texas, White spent months exposing corrupt police officers whom he caught red-handed selling back to peddlers the narcotics seized from them in raids. Two policemen, one a captain, went to prison and some officials tumbled from high places. When it was over a group of angry politicians turned on White, accusing him of being a Communist, a bold charge which they said was fully substantiated by his criticism of the police department. White's superiors quickly came to his defense and he left Texas with this significant comment:

"A crook is a crook whether or not he has a permit for the gun he carries in his pocket."

Today, in retirement after thirty-one years of service in the federal Narcotics Bureau, White divides his time between his San Francisco home, overlooking the bay, and a suburban beach cottage surrounded by flower gardens. He still points proudly to his Treasury Department medal and to a letter of praise written to him personally by President John F. Kennedy.

Of his achievements in the Bureau with eighteen years as a district supervisor, he takes a modest and philosophical view. "Greed is the same in many languages," he often says, "and a fat bankroll of American dollars can stimulate that greed better than anything else."

Chapter 7

Great Teigin Mystery
Tamegoro Ikii

Tamegoro Ikii, famed throughout Japan as one of the nation's ablest detectives, retired in 1964 at the age of sixty with the high rank of deputy chief of Tokyo's Metropolitan Police. With a record for solving 126 of the country's most baffling mysteries during his thirty-five years of service, he cherishes numbers of decorations and citations, including a sake cup presented to him personally by the Emperor's son from his own private collection.

The veteran officer, however, is proudest of his success in unraveling Japan's Great Teigin Mystery in which twelve men and women, employed in a bank, died of poison in a daring robbery, a case that has aroused intense interest in many foreign countries.

Ikii's achievements, like those of other famous detectives, demonstrate that the essential techniques of crime detection are the same in every land—perseverance, resourcefulness, keen powers of observation, and a deep understanding of human nature.

"In beginning an investigation," he says, "I have always made my mind clear like crystal with no advance opinions. At the scenes of crimes I have looked for little, hidden clues as well as large, obvious ones and in interrogating suspects I have watched their every movement—even of fingers and of eyes. From these you can often tell where the solution lies. And in reaching preliminary conclusions, I have found it essential to anticipate the next move or development—but if one makes a mistake in his first surmise, the next will probably be incorrect and the case will end in failure."

Useful as these procedures may be, Ikii often used them in interplay with another vital element—psychology. He seemed to know just how and when to touch the emotions of his suspects to make them introspective and soul-searching.

Such was the case in his investigation of a bold mail robbery on March 1, 1954, in a suburb of Yokohama when Eiichi Yokoyama, the twenty-two-year-old driver of a truck for the Japan Mail Transport Company, was waylaid by three armed men sitting in a sedan on a lonely road and robbed of mail valued at 194,882 yen, a considerable sum in those days.

Though the Transport Company was a private concern serving the government, the robbery brought public scorn upon the Postal Department which was accused of carelessness, and Yokohama authorities, believing that the robbers had come from Tokyo, asked that Ikii be put in charge of the manhunt.

After learning that the truck driver and his two companions had been kept locked in the bandits' car while the three holdup men drove the truck into the mountains to rifle the mail, Ikii reasoned that they had used a stolen sedan and later abandoned it. His widely broadcasted orders to hunt for such a machine led to a report on the following day that an auto of this description had been found in Yamanachi Prefecture and that a man, believed to have been the driver, was seen boarding a train for Tokyo. The license number of the car was found to be fictitious but by tracing numerals on the engine Ikii learned that it belonged to a United States Army officer, Major Robert W. Samuel, and that it had been stolen from in front of his home.

Reckoning that at least one of the robbers was from Tokyo

and that he probably had a record as a car thief, the detective ordered a search of files. Suspicion soon turned to one Teruo Kanzaki who had been in trouble for stealing cars and had vanished six years before while a sentence for theft was being appealed. The man was located and shadowed for days before his arrest. However, he vigorously denied any part in the mail robbery.

"While questioning him," Ikii recalls, "I watched every move he made—his shifting eyes, his twitching hands and I was certain that he was withholding the truth because of a troubled mind. I decided to use psychology and not to press him at once for a confession.

"Contemplating a very different approach, I sent an officer to Kanzaki's home village, Toyama, and we learned that he had been greatly worried over his family's poverty and their inability to send his youngest brother to high school. But now their circumstances had improved and the boy at last had gone to school.

"This I told our suspect, advising him to serve his term on the old charge; there no longer was need to worry about his family. At once I could see his anxiety slowly disappearing. He began to look like a different man. And after I had followed this tactic for a time, he broke down and confessed to the mail holdup, naming his confederates."

Most of the loot was recovered and Ikii received a citation from the head of Japan's Postal Department.

His work on a murder mystery was more difficult. The victim was Keiko Tijama, a maid for the American consul general in Tokyo, who was found strangled on the morning of May 1, 1953, in her room in a small annex in the consulate compound. Her bedroom had been rifled of money and valuables.

Because the victim was a Japanese, American military police called on Tokyo authorities for help and Ikii was assigned to the case. While many insisted that the killer was a consulate employee, Ikii was convinced that an outsider was responsible—a conclusion based on the apparent difficulty of the murderer in forcing open a window to gain entrance to the room and his care in wiping it to obliterate fingermarks.

Carefully examining the window, he discovered that two small prints had been overlooked but not until they had been compared with 40,000 fingerprints in police files were they found to match those of a man named Yoshida with a long record for thievery, but he had disappeared.

A hunt for Yoshida was failing when Ikii directed his men to look for two others known to be friends of the wanted man. One of them pointed out the fugitive in a Tokyo amusement park. Yoshida admitted the murder, stating that after he had gathered up the plunder the maid had awakened and he had strangled her to stifle her outcries. Ironically, he expressed remorse that his victim had been a Japanese, explaining that he had forced his way into the American compound because be always refused to break into the homes of his own countrymen.

Traditional love and respect for Japan's royal family have moved Ikii to place major importance on one of his cases involving far less effort than any of the others. "I am an old-time Japanese trained to have high regard for the imperial family," he relates, by way of introduction. "And so, when my country lost the war in 1945, my greatest concern was for this family. I suffered mentally when Prince Nashimoto Morisasa was imprisoned as a war criminal and I was happy when he was released four months later. His estate in Shibuya Ward of Tokyo had been bombed and his palace destroyed; only a storage house remained. Imagine then my feelings when robbers, in October 1947, broke into the storage house and carried away everything that it contained—160 items of clothing worth 81,100 yen.

"I was given charge of the case and naturally I determined to work my hardest. I called on the Prince and found him in the depths of despair. 'My home has been burned down,' he said sadly. 'Now all my belongings are gone. I don't even have an extra pair of socks. How will I live through the winter?'"

Ikii scrutinized the storage house for clues but found none. He concluded that his only hope lay in trying to trace the stolen clothing. With a number of men assisting him, he started a search of the hundreds of secondhand stores scattered throughout Tokyo. Four days later he located the shop where the loot had been sold by a Korean.

With tears in their eyes, the Prince and his wife thanked the detective and presented him with seven sake cups bearing the royal family insignia. Ikii kept one for himself and gave the others to the men who had helped him. "It was the first time in my career," he says now, "that I was ever thanked in such a manner—imagine such a thank you from royalty!"

The Great Teigin Mystery* which brought Ikii worldwide fame, began in Tokyo in the late afternoon of January 26, 1948, an hour after the Teikoku Bank's branch in the busy Shima-Machi District had closed for the day. Crowds of pedestrians were passing the rear entrance to the bank when a door suddenly swung open and a young woman in her early twenties, Masako Murata, staggered out into a lane. As she lay, writhing in pain, people rushed to her aid, inquiring what had happened, but she could only put her hand to her throat and mutter a single word—"poison."

Some ran to a nearby police box and an officer responded. Kneeling beside the prostrate girl, he tried to learn the cause of her condition. In response, she pointed feebly to the door of the bank and lapsed into unconsciousness.

As others sent for an ambulance, the policeman stepped

* Teigin means Imperial Bank. The name was changed after World War II when the Japanese sought to remove all vestiges of imperialism.

into the bank. Before him was a horrifying scene of death and agony. Stretched on the floor, wracked with convulsive pain, were men and women of all ages. Some appeared to be lifeless; others were moaning, and a few were frothing at the mouth.

Reaching for a telephone, he called the Majiro police station for help. "This looks like a very serious matter," he said. "About twelve people here in the bank have been stricken; some of them, I think, are dead. Ambulances have been summoned."

Officers were sent to the scene though the report at first did not arouse undue excitement at the station since food poisoning at this time was not unusual in Japan due to postwar food shortages and there were frequent deaths.

The actual seriousness of the situation was not realized until several hours later when medical officers, called to the emergency hospital, examined the victims and declared positively that they were not suffering from food poisoning but probably had swallowed a solution of cyanide of potassium, which usually causes immediate death. Shigeki Horizaki, the Chief of the Homicide Section of the Metropolitan Police, was advised of the gravity of the case and he hastened to the bank, accompanied by the Public Prosecutor, Umezo Takagi, of the Attorney General's Department. After cursory questioning of people in adjacent stores, none of whom could offer any explanation, the officials contacted the hospital and were told that of sixteen victims, ten had died almost instantly, two had succumbed during treatment, and that a remaining four were expected to survive.

Realizing that he faced a mystery of unusual proportions, Horizaki announced that he was assuming personal charge of the case and he dispatched large numbers of men to investigate, though nothing had yet been learned of the origin of the tragedy.

A careful search of the bank itself was fruitless; it revealed no clues, nor could the police learn whether money had been taken. "Could all this be some fatal accident?" the officers asked themselves. "Or is it deliberate murder?" There was no one to give an immediate answer.

Despite continuing investigation, it was not until late that night that the police received their first definite information. It came from the acting manager of the bank, Takijiro Yoshida, who had recovered sufficiently to make a statement, though doctors said that his condition still was critical.

"It was that man who came into the bank just as we were closing," he said, speaking faintly with obvious difficulty. "It was close to three-thirty. He walked in just as the doors were being shut. All of our people were quite busy, as they usually are at this time, so this man was led into my office and he . . ."

"Describe him quickly," Horizaki interrupted, fearing that his informant might lapse back into unconsciousness.

"He handed me a card—I think his name was Kato— and he said he came from the Welfare Ministry. He looked to be about forty; he was slim and his hair was cut quite short. He wore an arm band with one word on it—'Sanitation.'"

"Tell me, what did he say to you?" the officer pressed.

"Oh, yes, it comes back to me very clearly. He said that he had been instructed by the Health Section to disinfect the inside of the bank. I asked him why that was necessary and he explained that there had been an outbreak of dysentery in our area."

"And of course you told him to proceed, I presume," Horizaki interjected, knowing of the customary Japanese respect for authority.

The banker nodded. "Of course I did. Then he told me that before the disinfecting could start it would be necessary for all of us to take some medicine that he had with him— a drug that would immunize us against dysentery. Taken by mouth, he explained, was more effective than by injection.

"I watched him closely. He opened his bag and took out two bottles. I looked at them; they were labeled one and two. He also had a medical syringe.

"Naturally I wanted to cooperate, so I called to all of our staff to stop work and come into my office. I told them briefly the reason for this interruption and then the man took over with his own directions. He told . . ."

"Try and tell us in his own words if you can," the officer interrupted.

The manager wet his lips and it was evident that it was painful for him to speak. "As nearly as I can remember, this is what he said:

"'This medicine I'm giving you is very bad for the teeth so I must insist that you gulp it down in one swallow. I'll give you water from this other bottle to wash it down. Now all of you get your teacups and, please, hurry back.'

"The group broke up and when they returned they made a sort of circle around me, each person holding his cup in his hands. The man from the health office then put the end of his syringe in the bottle marked No. 1 and he filled each teacup, admonishing us not to drink until he told us to. He wanted us to drink all together.

"When the last of the cups had been filled, he told us to gulp it down and we obeyed. Then he quickly opened his second bottle—the one with the water—but already we were feeling a horrible burning in our throats. Some cried out for water; the man said that would do us no harm and most of us started for the kitchen—but I never got there. On the way everything went black—that's all I remember."

This was enough to convince Horizaki and his colleagues that they were face to face with a diabolical plot to do mass murder and they viewed the mystery as a challenge to the Metropolitan Police Department which only recently had been reorganized under American supervision during the occupation. There were no clues other than a description of the killer. However, motive was established when bank examiners found that 164,405 yen were missing from the bank together with a check for 17,405 yen. (At that time 360 yen were equivalent to one American dollar.)

Police proceeded on the theory that the murderer possessed some knowledge of medicine and was fairly well educated. Under this assumption, detectives were sent throughout the district with instructions to interview physicians, dentists, and druggists for any possible clues. At the same time a methodical check of criminal records was undertaken in the hope that they might disclose someone resembling the wanted man.

News of the tragedy created a sensation among the Japanese and there were strong demands on the police for quick and effective action.

Soon after the investigation was under way, the police learned from the Ebara Branch of the Yesuda Bank that about three months before, on October 14, 1947, it had been visited by a stranger under similar circumstances. He had said that he represented the Sanitation Section of the Welfare Ministry, and, with the permission of the bank manager, K. Astanabe, all of the staff had imbibed a liquid but no one had been stricken. The visitor had left a card bearing the name of Dr. Shigeru Matsui. Here, almost at the start, was what appeared to be a valuable clue but it soon collapsed when Dr. Matsui, a highly respected physician, came voluntarily to police headquarters, identified the card as his, and had no difficulty in convincing the officers that he in no way was involved or knew anything about the case. Obviously, his card could have come into possession of the killer in many ways.

There also was another early development; the Nakai Branch of the Mitsubishi Bank reporting that on January 19 of the same year, only a week before the tragedy, a man of the same description had called there on a like mission but manager Taizo Ogawa had told him that everyone was busy and that he should return later. Promising to do so, he had left a card. It bore the name of Jiro Yamaguchi which in Japan is as common as John Smith is in America. However, this was no time to overlook a lead of any kind.

Search for the murderer led to the Suginami Ward of Tokyo where detectives found a man named Yoneo Itatano who fitted the description of the poisoner, even to the closely cropped hair. He had once used the alias of Jiro Yamaguchi and for a time it appeared that the hunt might be over but Itatano produced an alibi that could not be shaken. There were plenty of other Yamaguchis to be questioned and they were located one after another.

Oddly, the interrogation of so many Yamaguchis in widely scattered parts of Japan provided something of a humorous note to what otherwise was stark tragedy, but before long every available person of that name had been eliminated. One Jiro Yamaguchi, a prominent lumberman, was so incensed by loss of business through newspaper publicity, that he offered a large reward for apprehension of the murderer.

The next important development occurred four days later when Horizaki was advised that the check for 17,405 yen, stolen from the bank, had been located in the Itabashi Bank where it had been cashed a day after the tragedy by a man who wore dark glasses and hurried away without stopping to count the currency. The cashier could not describe him.

By January 31, five days after the bank had been robbed, the four surviving employees had recovered sufficiently to meet at police headquarters to view photographs of known criminals. They spent hours comparing pictures but no one could agree that any single person actually resembled the man who had given them the poison. However, their detailed descriptions prompted a police artist to draw a composite picture which all agreed looked like the wanted man. It soon appeared on circulars which were distributed by the thousands.

Late that night, Horizaki, working on a new clue in the

outskirts of Tokyo, telephoned metropolitan headquarters in great excitement. He had just arrested a man named Kansako Otsuka and he believed that a confession was imminent. This man, he reported, had been in prison for fraud, having posed as a former major in the Army Medical Corps. Since his release he was known to be impoverished but on the day following the murders he had been seen spending money freely.

Otsuka was taken to headquarters and questioned for hours on his alibi which finally was completely verified and the authorities were obliged to let him go.

There were other suspects as days of intensive work continued but in each instance high hopes collapsed. In desperation the police, still pressed by the public for a solution, created a special department to devote itself entirely to this case. People read the news with a critical eye and condemnation of the police mounted fast, becoming increasingly severe as distribution of more and more of the descriptive circulars brought about the arrest of suspects by the score.

Equally unsuccessful was the laborious and far-reaching questioning of every man who had served in the Army Medical Corps during the war. It was a task engaging a large detail of picked men who moved from one part of the country to another, but their efforts produced only one suspect resembling the fugitive and his alibi could not be shaken.

Now badly frustrated, the police hierarchy turned to another tack. Since the personal card of the well-known Dr. Matsui had been left by the murderer in one of the banks, the officers reckoned that it would be well to ascertain how many of his cards he had given away and to whom, the Japanese being accustomed to exchanging business and calling cards.

The doctor told them that some months before a printer had supplied him with a hundred professional cards; all of them had been given out and Dr. Matsui soon found himself facing a difficult and time-consuming task.

"To whom did you give all of these cards?" the detectives had inquired.

The doctor merely shrugged his shoulders. "Mostly to patients," he finally explained. "I hand them out with a notation of the next appointment—but I've given some to other people in exchange for their cards as we are in the habit of doing."

"Then we'll have to ask you to do something for us no matter how much time it takes," the police told him. "It is of the greatest importance that we know the name of each and every person to whom you gave your cards. Check your list of patients; check the cards that you've received from other people in exchange for yours. We'll be back in a few days."

Working conscientiously for hours, the doctor finally completed a list of each of the one hundred persons who had received his cards. It was a trying task but he fully understood the seriousness of his assignment.

With the names in their possession, the investigators turned at once to checking every individual, some in Tokyo and others in distant cities. February and March passed with no indication of success. Fully fifty of the cards had been checked and the individuals eliminated. There still remained another half hundred people to be located.

One of the top names on Dr. Matsui's list had been that of Sadamichi Hirasawa, a noted artist, with whom the doctor had exchanged cards while riding with him on a ferry. The card bore an address in Nakano Ward and although some considered it a waste of time, a detective was sent there to interview Hirasawa.

On the officer's return he reported that his trip had been a useless expense of time and money. The artist, he said, was ten years older than the approximate age of the murderer; moreover, the detective explained that a thorough check of Hirasawa's background had revealed that the man was highly recognized in the art world, his paintings being accepted for exhibit without even the usual formality of being shown first to examining committees. Without question, Hirasawa was eliminated along with the others who had been visited.

When April came with still no sign of progress, a conference of top police officials from all parts of Japan was held in Tokyo and for days every scrap of information on the case was thoroughly rechecked. Painstakingly, the officers read and reread reports concerning the individuals to whom Dr. Matsui had given his cards and it was decided that all of them should be questioned for a second time. During the discussion, the artist, Hirasawa, was mentioned. Most of those present argued that it would be an imposition to again disturb a man of his prominence but in the end it was agreed that no exceptions should be made.

Reports of the renewed interviews trickled into headquarters but, as before, there was nothing to indicate that any of these people even remotely could be connected with the crime, nor could they be of any help in solving it.

Another conference of the same officials took place and attention turned once more to the disappointing task of checking Dr. Matsui's cards. By this time eighty-four of them had been finally eliminated; only sixteen remained to be checked and those involved were in distant areas. There was scant hope that these would be any more productive than the others, yet all believed that at the moment there was no alternative but to continue this frustrating procedure.

The discussion had continued for a time when one of the men interrupted with a question. "Just why hasn't Tamegoro Ikii been called into this case?" he demanded. "He's worked on so many of our most difficult situations and he never quits until he has a solution. I'm telling you, the man has some kind of a sixth sense—and he uses it to get results."

"He's been considered for this job before," another interjected. "But they keep saying that he's busy with some other very important government matter."

In the end it was decided to call on the police high command with a request that Ikii be relieved of all other duties and given free rein in trying to solve the Teigin Mystery. The request was granted and Ikii, a powerfully-built man, with graying hair and peering eyes, was summoned. He listened eagerly as the case was outlined and his eyes lighted as if he were being asked to do something that no one else had ever undertaken. To him it was a brand-new challenge.

"I'd like to start by visiting Dr. Matsui and discussing the cards—and the people who got them," he said after some thought.

Some of his listeners tried to conceal cynical smiles. "He's been talked to at least a dozen times and by almost as many men," one officer asserted.

"But I really would like to meet him myself," Ikii insisted. "You've given me a difficult assignment and I believe I should be permitted to proceed in my own way."

There being no substantial objections, he was told to pursue his own course and in a few days he was conversing with the doctor who said frankly that he believed he already had given the police all of the help he could. Nevertheless, Ikii insisted on reviewing each of the eighty-four cards that had been checked and discussing each individual. Hirasawa's name was among them and for reasons which the physician could not understand the detective seemed more interested in him than in all the others.

"He's a man of unimpeachable reputation," Dr. Matsui insisted. "If this were my case, he'd be the first man I'd eliminate."

Ikii shrugged his shoulders. "I simply cannot tell you why," he said, speaking deliberately, "but in spite of everything, I want to talk to him myself—and in my own way."

"A hunch perhaps?" the other asked, laughing.

"Call it that if you wish; but I'd rather just say intuition. Don't ask me why—if you did I couldn't tell you but something tells me it's the thing I should do."

"You're a detective; I'm just a doctor." And the interview ended.

Guided by his impulse, Ikii went to the artist's home and explained his mission. Their talk had not proceeded far before the detective realized that probably he had not come in vain.

"The man's appearance struck me immediately," he told his superiors some time later. "Although he is fifty-seven years of age, he could easily pass for forty-five and when I looked at him closely, I was surprised to find how much he resembled our composite picture of the poisoner. I really wonder why no one ever noticed it before. Perhaps the difference in age threw them off the track."

He went on to say that he had stealthily taken the picture from his pocket in the artist's presence. "The resemblance was simply startling," he said.

There was still another factor that had puzzled the detective. While Ikii, speaking with extreme caution, had stressed that his visit was prompted only by a hope that Hirasawa might have some theory of his own, the artist had volunteered an alibi, explaining with obvious care that on the day of the murders he was attending an art exhibit in Tokyo.

Traveling home, Ikii found himself deeply perplexed and the more he reviewed the conversation the more suspicious he became. "There was just something fishy about the way he talked and acted," Ikii said later, "but I couldn't put my finger on it—and I still can't."

The more he pondered the situation, the more convinced Ikii became that the painter knew more than he was telling. Half way on his return to headquarters, he had decided to turn about and call on Hirasawa again. The artist greeted him with obvious surprise. "I thought you had returned to

Tokyo," he commented. "Did you overlook something in our talk?"

Ikii laughed. "No, indeed," he said casually. "I was delayed in leaving and I wanted you to know how very much I appreciate the time you spent with me. I've come to ask you to be my guest at dinner tonight."

With apparent relief, the artist accepted and that night the two enjoyed a sumptuous meal in one of the city's most popular restaurants. In his own way, Ikii had arranged to have the restaurant's attractive girl photographer come to their table and while she stood before them with poised camera, the detective laughingly suggested that they have their picture taken "just as a souvenir of my visit with a famous artist."

Ikii kept his eyes on his guest as the camera snapped and he observed the other deliberately distorting his face just before the shutter snapped. He proposed a second "shot" and this time Hirasawa quickly lowered his chin to his breast in an obvious attempt to conceal his features from the camera.

The detective started home in high spirits, convinced this time that he had found the wanted man and that it remained only to further tighten the case before arresting him. He was wholly unprepared for the reaction of his superiors.

Although he showed them the photographs of Hirasawa, taken at the restaurant, pointing out the close resemblance to the composite picture, they told him bluntly that they already had eliminated the artist and under no circumstances would they even consider involving him in the case. Ikii's arguments failed and he finally walked away chagrined and disappointed. He had not reckoned with a new sense of democracy and civil rights that had come upon the Japanese as a result of American occupation.

The months-long questioning of hundreds of people by the police had run counter to the new social consciousness of the people and they were crying out against what they termed as invasions of their rights. The old order had changed. Newspapers, responsive to public opinion, had taken up the issue and in spite of their earlier demands for action, they now reversed themselves, accusing the police of overzealously resorting to Gestapo-like tactics. In such a climate, the police were in no mood to arrest a nationally known artist with the possibility that he might be vindicated.

Ikii, on the other hand, could not be persuaded to abandon the case. Risking censure, he resolved to weave a net of incriminating evidence about his suspect for now, reason rather than intuition, told him that Hirasawa was the man who had poured the lethal potions in the bank.

Working secretly and alone, he first ascertained when Hirasawa would be away from home. Then, availing himself of this opportunity, he called on the artist's wife with no hint of his purpose. The information that he received required long and careful checking, but when Ikii had finished he had in his possession a mass of damning facts.

He had learned that two days before January 26 when the murders occurred, Hirasawa had been unable to pay a bill of 150 yen, while a week later his wife had deposited 44,500 yen in a bank; that soon afterward he had given her 69,000 yen to keep for him.

This, however, was not all. He ascertained further that for some time the artist had been maintaining two mistresses in luxurious apartments and that shortly before the crime he had found himself hard pressed for money.

Other evidence as important was assembled and Ikii, with characteristic determination, called again on high officers of the metropolitan police. He told them what he had learned and requested that a warrant be obtained for the man's arrest. This time he was successful.

Late in August, seven months after the crime, Ikii left for Hirasawa's home and placed him under arrest, though the man bitterly insisted that he was not guilty. Returning triumphantly to Tokyo with his prisoner handcuffed to two policemen, Ikii soon found himself the center of denunciation by the press. That a man of Hirasawa's stature should be humiliated by handcuffs was more than most newsmen could comprehend and they spared no words in saying so. Editorials supported their position, accusing the detective of violating the new constitution and of flaunting newly acquired civil rights. In response, Ikii simply stated that it was his responsibility to bring Hirasawa back alive and that he had done his duty in the way that he saw fit.

Meanwhile the accused man had been taken to police headquarters and paraded before the four survivors of the poisoning plot. Of this number only one would identify him positively, though all said that he "could" be the man. Somewhat disappointed, Ikii led his prisoner into a private room where questioning began in the presence of high officials.

"Where did you get all your money?" Ikii first demanded, carefully avoiding any mention of the looted bank.

"From the president of the Imo Industrial Company, Mr. Ugo Hanada," the artist shot back.

"When?"

"In October of last year."

"How much did you get?"

"Two hundred thousand yen."

"Are you certain it was in October of last year—not before?"

"Positive."

Ikii jumped to his feet, an accusing finger pointed at the prisoner. "In October of last year," he shouted, "Ugo Hanada was in his grave."

Hirasawa paled. "I guess it must have been in October of the year before," he countered.

"Where did you get the money you gave your wife last February?" the detective pressed.

"From an old friend who paid a debt. He first wired me that he was sending the money and then it came—a few days later, I believe."

Ikii was on his feet again. "I've seen that wire and I've checked it," he exclaimed. "You sent that telegram to yourself so you could show it to your wife and explain where the money came from. Now didn't you?"

Hirasawa did not answer.

He was shown Dr. Matsui's calling card that had been presented by the medicine man on his visit to one of the other banks before the tragedy. Hirasawa admitted that it once had been in his possession but he had a ready explanation. "It was stolen from my overcoat pocket in late last May."

"Don't you know that no one wears an overcoat in late May?" Ikii shot back. "Don't you know that May is too hot for overcoats?"

Again the prisoner stared back in silence and he was taken to a cell.

Ikii, however, had not yet completed his investigation. He made another trip to Hirasawa's home and searched it thoroughly. In a desk he found a bank book in the name of one Kuchi Hayashi showing a deposit of 80,000 yen two days after the murders. Adding this to the money already accounted for, the detective calculated that it would approximately account for the stolen funds, presuming that the robber had kept a considerable amount for his personal use.

Hirasawa was confronted with these new facts and again he had an explanation. "Hayashi is a friend of mine," he said. "We were involved in a business deal and I gave him the money to deposit in his account."

Hayashi, however, had a different story. He told Ikii that his bank book had been stolen from him by a pickpocket in Tokyo and emphatically denied that he had ever made the 80,000 yen deposit.

Hirasawa was charged with murder and as questioning continued it appeared that he was nearing the breaking point. Not until late in October, however, did he finally admit that he was cornered and he made a full confession. The police had spent 6,000,000 yen on the long investigation, far more than any other single investigation had ever cost, and they calculated that a total of 8796 individuals had been questioned.

Hirasawa, revealing the motive for the crime, told Ikii that supporting his wife and two mistresses had drained him of his savings and that he was heavily in debt. He said that he had purchased cyanide to use in a new type of water color paint he was developing and had finally decided to put it to another purpose. Ikii then inquired into the visits to two other banks and the artist explained that in those instances he had diluted the poison into far too weak a solution.

The long hunt for the murderer appeared to be at an end but unexpectedly Hirasawa repudiated his confession, insisting that it had been made under duress; that the police had denied him sleep until he was forced to admit the guilt. Then he told a rambling story about his mind occasionally going blank since 1925 when he received inoculations against rabies. It was in such a state of mental aberration, he insisted, that he had confessed.

The case dragged through the courts for months. It was the first major trial since the change of Japanese governmental structure and great emphasis was given to the defendant's presumption of innocence. The Medical Department of Tokyo was called on to examine the accused. On April 7, 1950, psychiatrists reported to the court that he was sane when the crime was committed and that the rabies injections could not have caused mental derangement.

Again there were long delays over technicalities but on July 25, 1950, two and a half years after the crime, Hirasawa was convicted of first-degree murder and sentenced to be hanged. He was taken to Miyagi Prison, a federal penitentiary equipped for executions, and it was expected that his death would follow shortly but the case was not to end so quickly.

Despite earlier bitter reactions to the crime with demands for quick capture and punishment of the murderer, sentiment in some quarters turned in Hirasawa's favor and many people, influenced by Japan's new social changes, pleaded for his life. Some continued to accuse the police of violating civil rights. Their cause was joined by opponents of the death penalty and a new organization soon emerged, the Society to Help Hirasawa.

Under these pressures, the Minister of Justice decided to withhold the signing of a death warrant and his successors have done likewise.

Years passed and the condemned man's sympathizers engaged an attorney, Isamu Zuzuki, to continue the fight. Word came long afterward that a fisherman, Harumichi Nomura, who had once resided in Satagaya Ward, had vital information in Hirasawa's favor but he had moved and no one knew where he was. The search went on for months until the man was located. He was eager to reveal that late in October 1947 he had visited Hirasawa at his home and had paid him 150,000 yen for sixteen paintings. On a second visit in April of the following year, he said, he had bought several other pictures for 40,000 yen.

The defense made much of this disclosure, arguing that it partially accounted for the artist's money but the prosecution insisted that it was of no relevance since it did not concern the large sums Hirasawa had deposited in a bank and given to his wife within days of the murders.

The defense society, failing on this point, continued its investigation. In 1965 it came forward with two new witnesses in Hirasawa's behalf but the Supreme Court, after granting him a rehearing, finally rejected his appeal and reaffirmed the death sentence. The two new witnesses were indicted for perjury.

At this writing Hirasawa, now seventy-six years of age, still occupies a death cell in Miyagi Prison. Many predict that his death there will cheat the law.

Chapter 8

War on the Mafia

Joseph Petrosino

On a sad day in late March of 1909, New York City paid
a great and most touching tribute to a martyred police
officer. More than 200,000 people lined the streets along the
route of a mile-long funeral cortege. Many others stood on
balconies or looked through windows. All bared their heads
and bowed as the hearse passed slowly by, drawn by six
horses draped in white. In the casket lay the body of one
of the city's most famous and beloved detectives, Lieutenant Joseph Petrosino, who had been ruthlessly shot down
in Sicily while on a secret mission to investigate the Mafia
and to learn who of its members were coming to America.

For years he had warred relentlessly and without fear
against these terrorists in New York and other large American cities. It was a campaign to which he was devoutly
dedicated, not only in line of duty but with the broader
and nobler purpose of protecting his countrymen from foreign criminals who preyed upon immigrant families. To
his credit was a record of more than five hundred convictions, some for murder, and the deportation of an equal
number.

His tragic death on the night of March 12, 1909, shocked
the western world and brought grief to half a million Italians in New York who had looked to him alone as their
protector. Flags flew at half-mast from public and private
buildings on the day of the funeral and city officials led

the procession as it moved from old St. Patrick's Cathedral on Mott Street to the grave in Calvary Cemetery. In the opinion of many it was a demonstration remarkable for its sincerity and its spontaneous expressions of sorrow and respect.

Today, more than half a century later, yellowed files relate in the stereotyped words of official reports the career of this clever and courageous officer who had battled against overwhelming odds to crush the Mafia and the Camorra while their leaders were laying the foundations of today's national crime syndicates. They tell of his success in many cases such as his capture of a desperate extortionist who once had selected Enrico Caruso, the great Italian tenor, for his victim. And they reveal how, by ingenious disguises and daring strategy, he penetrated the headquarters of Black Hand terrorists to arrest their leaders. The story of his accomplishments, however, should be told from its beginning.

He was born in 1860 in the coastal town of Salerno near Naples at a time when much of Italy and Sicily was infested by the Mafia and the Camorra which began many years before as secret patriotic societies only to be taken over by desperate criminals. The two fraternities long afterward were to be merged into one dreaded society—the Mafia.

His parents, like many of their townsmen, had lived in constant fear of these demanding elements and when life became unbearable they sought refuge in America. Young Joseph was six years old when they reached New York and settled in that part of Manhattan's Lower East Side known as Little Italy.

The boy, musically inclined, was given lessons on the harp until the family's dwindling resources interfered and he was obliged to shine shoes after school. Some years later, with grade school behind him, he obtained his first job as a street sweeper. Already a hard worker, always ambitious, he was advanced to foreman. In time Police Inspector Alexander Williams took notice of the authoritative manner in which the young man directed his crew and told him that he should become a policeman. Petrosino declined, explaining that he liked his job and planned to keep it.

This he probably would have done had he not listened, with mounting concern, to the troubles of his countrymen suffering at the hands of Black Hand gangsters. Murders were not infrequent and it became increasingly apparent that immigrants like himself were falling victims of the criminals from whom they had tried to escape. He resolved to turn to law enforcement for the sake of those who needed protection.

Now twenty-three years of age and a naturalized citizen, he applied for a place on the police force and was appointed October 9, 1883. He was dark and stocky, tipping the scales at 200. He measured only five feet and seven inches, but he was all muscle and in his face there was a look of fearlessness. He had a way of staring at people and at things with a dull expression and an air of amiable simplicity. Later, as a detective, it would enable him to mingle with crowds without attracting undue attention.

For a time he walked a beat and brother officers often looked curiously at the husky rookie who spoke English with a pronounced Italian accent. Throughout his life he was to move in circles where Italian was spoken almost exclusively.

In these early years he kept mostly to himself but his superiors were attracted by his close attention to duty. Meritorious reports filtered into headquarters, bringing promotion to the detective division. As he was assigned to cases involving Mafia violence, he resolved to study the history and inner workings of the mysterious brotherhood of which he had little knowledge beyond what he had been told by his parents and had learned scantily in New York.

Delving far into the past, he found that the Mafia, which

in later years had produced such criminals as "Scarface" Al Capone, Albert Anastasia, "Lucky" Luciano, and Frank Costello, had its beginning in the mid-eighteenth century, though some Sicilians still believe that it started many years before. It was originally a loosely organized fraternity of Sicilian families created to combat the brutality of the island's Bourbon rulers. A member became known as a *mafioso*, meaning a shrewd man who knew how to use a gun and stood ready to rescue a brother even at the risk of life or fortune; one who would consider a wrong against a brother by any outsider as a wrong against himself.

Silence was an inviolate rule with a pledge never to admit the existence of the brotherhood or to appeal to police or courts for redress of wrongs. It had no president or other officers, nor were there dues or by-laws save those unwritten ones which were to pass from one generation to another. In such a society might was right and the gun became the law as it still is among Mafia members today.

Gradually, the *mafiosi*, as they are known, turned to crime as a way of livelihood and when the wave of Italian immigration to America started in 1880, members of the society soon learned that there were fertile fields in the fast-growing colonies of their countrymen in New York, Chicago, New Orleans, and other cities.

Word of fabulous profits soon trickled overseas to the fatherland, inducing others to join the trek to the New World. Italian shopkeepers and farmers, aware that the Mafia meant business, became easy victims. A note signed with the unmistakable Black Hand, the warning of death, would accompany a demand for money. If ignored, there came a second warning—but never a third. Usually the victim paid; otherwise his store would be bombed or he might be shot from ambush or be found with his throat cut. For the Mafia it was rich business; for the police it provided almost insurmountable problems.

With success, the Mafia acquired greater power and

mounting arrogance. Its operations spread westward, finally to San Francisco where many Italians had settled. To a far less degree, with steadily diminishing strength, the society still exists today, despite modern methods of law enforcement and in defiance of police vigilance.

From his studies Petrosino became fully aware of the nature of the enemy he had sworn to fight. He knew its ways and the dangers that lurked in his path but he was not afraid. Those who dared to abuse the freedom of America became his foes.

In his early investigations he had found it difficult and often impossible to obtain information. Victims naturally kept their silence in fear of retaliation; too many informers already had paid the penalty. Far from discouraged, he turned to disguises and to clever ruses that gradually saved many from Black Hand extortion. Word of his accomplishments became known among immigrants and they slowly began to trust this courageous young detective and to bring him information.

He worked so secretly that he often was passed unrecognized by his own brother officers. In time he was appointed to head a small but special group of picked detectives known as the Italian Squad. Assuming his new post, he knew that he must find a way for safe communication with his countrymen when trouble came; to be seen walking into police headquarters would be nothing less than suicide.

Petrosino met the problem by establishing secret meeting places in scattered areas far from police stations where Mafia victims could come in safety. One such rendezvous was on Waverly Place on the outskirts of Greenwich Village where few Italians lived. The plan achieved its purpose but it once gave the detective unexpected difficulty. A patrolman had watched suspiciously as men with furtive looks hurried into the place in late night hours, and he told his captain that he had uncovered the headquarters of a gang of anarchists. A raid followed and among those hustled into a patrol wagon was Petrosino in laborer's clothes. On the way to the station house he identified himself and was released together with the others who had come to him for help.

He usually tried to avoid making arrests; instead, he directed men of his squad or of other commands to take prisoners into custody, for he realized that becoming well known to criminals would impair his usefulness. However, when it did become necessary for him to act alone, he was not one to pound a door and demand admittance. He just drew his gun and broke in.

One of the squad's most lasting contributions was its growing file of records and photographs of Italian and Sicilian criminals in America and overseas. It filled a want that had impeded the police for years before Petrosino recognized the need and prepared to meet it.

He gradually became a vast reservoir of information. He knew the habits of hundreds of men and significant facts about their ways. How all of this was accumulated no one fully knew, though he admitted that he learned much by moving about in disguise.

For such maneuvers he would discard his customary hard black derby hat, replacing it with a peaked cap or a worn brown felt hat with a wide brim pulled over his eyes. Wearing a long, shabby overcoat and a red bandanna carelessly tied around his neck, he would trudge in and out of wine shops on the Lower East Side. Sometimes he would disappear for days, returning with dirty, calloused hands from digging ditches with laborers who had information to impart. Occasionally, when a situation demanded, he would pose as an immigration officer or a health inspector.

In the summer of 1896, a new and more menacing wave of crime swept through New York's Little Italy. Black Hand warnings appeared with increasing frequency and extortion notes demanding money under penalty of kidnaping or death, became almost a daily occurrence. Petrosino knew at once that the Mafia was spreading out but the challenge was too great for the little group of men under his command. He discussed the situation with Commissioner Theodore Bingham, then head of the Police Department, and the formation of a larger and more powerful secret service squad was planned, only to encounter political opposition. Necessary funds were refused by the authorities but private citizens and organizations, recognizing the need, came forward with substantial contributions. When all obstacles had been swept aside, Petrosino was summoned to Bingham's office.

"You are to be in complete command," the commissioner told the swarthy little detective. "Pick your own men—fifty of them; take them from anywhere in the department or even from out of it. They will work under your command."

The detail, as finally created, was a group of shrewd, hard-fisted trustworthy men all of whom spoke Italian fluently. Its personnel was known only to Bingham and to Petrosino.

Before long Petrosino's courage and resourcefulness became legend throughout New York. Newspapers took note of his achievements and gave unstinting praise. The *New York Times* once had this to say:

> When murder and blackmail are in the air and the men folks are white-faced but swearing and the women folk are saying litanies to the Blessed Mother that their dark-haired cherub children may be saved from the Black Hand kidnappers, a telephone call comes to Police Headquarters in Mulberry Street for Petrosino and all Little Italy looks to the Italian detective for protection.

Typical of his operations was his reaction to a rumor that Enrico Alfano, a desperate leader of the Mafia, had arrived in New York from Naples where he was wanted for the murder of a man and wife.

Petrosino first found an informant who had seen the fu-

gitive in Italy and could describe him well. Then he undertook to search the underworld for days and finally located
Alfano in a dingy cellar dive on Mulberry Street. Quickly
rounding up several of his men, he posted them at the door
while he walked into the place alone and found his quarry
seated in the back of a gas-lit room, surrounded by gunmen
who had gathered to pay him homage, knowing that he had
come to America to weld the Mafia into a more powerful
underworld force.

While the detectives at the door looked on anxiously,
fearing that someone would lunge at the squatty detective,
Petrosino approached the man and dropped a heavy hand
on his shoulder.

"You're under arrest," he said in a loud voice, ringing with
authority. "You will be held for the authorities in Naples."

Alfano stared helplessly at those around him but they
seemed stunned by the courage of the lone officer and
kept their places. The Neapolitan, manacled, walked out
meekly in Petrosino's custody. He was deported in chains to
Naples. Months later Petrosino received a gold watch from
the Italian consul with a note of congratulation. They became his most treasured possessions.

New York police were still discussing the detective's courage when Rafaelo Palizzolo, another desperate figure in the
Mafia, slipped into the city. Petrosino learned of it, traced
him to his haunts, and ordered him out of New York.
Palizzolo packed his bags and left as quietly as he had
come.

Some time later attempts were made to assassinate members of Europe's royal families and the United States Secret
Service became worried over the safety of President William
McKinley. Petrosino was called on to obtain what information he could.

Posing as an active anarchist, he worked his way into
secret organizations in New York and in Paterson, New
Jersey but without result. Then, disguising himself as an

Italian immigrant, he went to Ellis Island, circulating among newcomers who were being held by federal authorities on suspicion of anarchistic affiliations. Slowly he learned of a plot, hatched by fanatics, to murder the rulers of every country in the western world. He warned the Secret Service that the President was marked for death and urged that he be not permitted to appear in public before large crowds.

His warning went unheeded and President McKinley fell from an assassin's bullet at the Pan-American Exposition in Buffalo, New York, on September 6, 1901. At the news Petrosino burst into tears. "Why didn't they listen to me?" he asked sorrowfully.

Of the many cases illustrating Petrosino's unusual resourcefulness and courage, two stand out among all others. One involves an extortion plot against the great Enrico Caruso; the other is still known as "the sugar barrel murder."

The famous tenor became a victim of the Mafia at a time when the blackmailers, hungry for money, had turned from poor hard-working immigrants to men of influence and popularity. In New York for an operatic engagement, Caruso was alarmed to find himself the recipient of a Black Hand letter demanding $5000. He was warned not to contact the police and there were detailed instructions as to how and where the money was to be delivered.

Caruso thought at once of his good friend, Lieutenant Petrosino, and hastened to his office with the letter, eager for both advice and protection. Though Caruso's first inclination was to pay the money, Petrosino cautioned him that if he did more and greater demands would follow.

"But if I don't pay and they find out I've been to the police my life won't be worth a penny," Caruso argued.

"Let me handle this in my own way," the detective told him. "You'll have no cause for worry."

When the singer left the office, followed to his hotel by a plainclothesman, Petrosino sat down to think. He read and reread the letter and finally a plan evolved. It demonstrated again that the detective, often obvious and impulsive in his approach, could be subtle when a situation warranted. He chose to lure the extortionist into a position where he could be captured without ever knowing that he had been suspected.

Hours later a man who looked like an Italian junk peddler was seen trudging along in the Lower East Side. Thus disguised, Petrosino looked hopefully for a clue that would uncover a suspect. He walked in and out of bars, talked to strangers and listened to many conversations. But days passed without a successful clue to the extortionist's identity.

Rereading the Black Hand letter, Petrosino noted again that it directed Caruso to wrap the money in brown paper and leave it under the stairway in the hall of a designated East Side tenement house. Whistling softly, he slapped his knees as an idea went flashing through his fertile mind.

That night, when the members of the Secret Service Squad assembled, he scanned them carefully, finally selecting one who somewhat resembled the great tenor. "You and I have a rather difficult job to do," he told the man. "Meet me in the morning. I'll have some clothes and a wig for you to wear. You're going to impersonate Enrico Caruso."

This, however, was only half of the plan. He picked three more men, instructing them to report the next morning in different garb—one as a street sweeper, another dressed like a lineman, and a third as a truck driver. Plans were meticulously discussed.

At the appointed time, the detective resembling Caruso went to the tenement and placed a bulky package in brown paper under the stairway as the letter had instructed. Outside a detective was busily pushing a broom along the curb. A second squad man was working with his pliers about a telephone pole, scaling it at times. A short distance away, three other detectives crouched in a parked truck, while another assumed the role of driver.

They did not have long to wait. Soon a shabbily dressed

man stepped from inside a doorway and walked cautiously down the street. He darted to the stairway, picked up the dummy parcel and started off.

Petrosino, hidden in an adjoining dwelling, gave a signal and the detectives went into action. The "street sweeper" drew a revolver and the "lineman" pulled a pair of handcuffs from his overalls. The man with the package was taken without trouble.

He said his name was Giuseppe Calabonna but he would not tell by whom he had been sent. His sentence was ten years in prison for extortion.

Caruso complimented his detective friend but feared that he again might suffer Black Hand threats or more brutal treatment. Police in plain clothes guarded him for months but he was not molested.

The sugar barrel murder, as it is still referred to, was of a far different nature but like the Caruso case it further illustrated Petrosino's tenacity and ingenious methods. This time the detective failed to obtain a conviction because terrified witnesses had disappeared but, for the police, in a legal sense the case was closed and his work resulted in what was generally regarded as a moral triumph of justice.

On the afternoon of April 14, 1903, a woman walking alone over Eleventh Avenue in New York City glanced into an old barrel behind a pile of lumber. She screamed at the gruesome sight that met her eyes and ran for a policeman. Wedged in the barrel was the murdered body of a man.

The victim had been stabbed thirteen times and the head was almost completely severed from the body. Because the nature of the crime clearly indicated the work of the Mafia, the case was assigned to Petrosino. The special squads had not yet been organized.

First he carefully examined the barrel with a magnifying glass. Tiny grains of white sugar adhered to the inside seams. He scraped the bottom and found a bit of sawdust. Meagre as they were, these did provide initial clues.

The dead man's trousers yielded a small crucifix. In his vest pocket was a watch chain but no watch and in a coat pocket the detective found the crumpled portion of an unsigned note apparently written by a woman.

Petrosino turned again to the barrel looking for further clues. On the inside of the stays he observed a notation— W & T 233. With nothing more to guide him he went to work.

The barrel markings led him to the wholesale grocery firm of Wallace & Thompson where he learned that careful records were kept of all barrels sent out. The one in question, filled with sugar, had been delivered to a wineshop at 226 Elizabeth Street.

That address was familiar to Petrosino, who had long suspected it as a rendezvous for counterfeiters and Mafia leaders. Dressing in his shabbiest clothes and with dirt smeared on his hands and face, he started for the shop. At the door he was seen to stagger and he saw to it that he walked unsteadily to the counter. "A bottle of the cheapest red you got," he ordered and while the clerk was reaching for a shelf Petrosino observed a thin sprinkling of sawdust on the floor. He asked himself whether it might match the scrapings taken from the barrel.

He bent down, pretending to tie his shoe, and slyly slipped a pinch of sawdust into the cuff of his trouser leg. Loud talk was coming from a back room and the detective, straining his ears, heard someone say that Giuseppe Morello had been seen there the previous day talking to Tomasso Petto who was spending money freely. Petrosino had never heard of Petto but he knew Morello to be the leader of a Mafia gang.

Returning to his office, he emptied his trouser cuff and sent the sawdust to an expert together with his scant specimen from the barrel. On examination the two samples proved to be identical.

On the next day he assembled members of his squad and

raided the wineshop, arresting everyone in the place. One of them was Tomasso Petto who drew a knife in an attempt to stab Petrosino but the officer disarmed him and snapped handcuffs on his wrists. When the man was searched, a pawn ticket was found in his coat pocket. Petto had pawned a watch. Later it proved to have been taken from the murder victim.

Meanwhile every effort to identify the dead man had failed. On a chance, Petrosino ordered the seven men taken in the raid to be driven to the morgue but as each was shown the body he merely shook his head, insisting that he had never seen the victim. Petrosino was discouraged and for a time he feared that the murdered man might never be identified, but he was not one to ever leave a murder unsolved.

Believing that he should know more about Morello and Petto, he inquired about their movements and was told that they were often seen in company of a barber who was treasurer of a defense fund being raised in behalf of a counterfeiter, Giuseppe de Priemo, then serving fourteen years in Sing Sing prison. The fund was to be used in a fight for a new trial.

He learned further that de Priemo, in his hopes for freedom, had become discouraged, fearing that he had been deserted by his underworld associates.

The prison became the detective's next destination. He sat down with the convict and convinced him that his friends actually had lost all interest in the case. Then he casually reached into his pocket for a picture of the dead man, snapped at the morgue, and showed it to de Priemo, explaining that he had been the victim of a hit-run driver.

"Why that's my brother-in-law, Benditto Madonna," the prisoner exclaimed. "He came here to see me only two months ago."

"What did you talk about?" Petrosino pressed.

"I asked him to find a fellow named Giuseppe Morello and get my money away from him."

"What money?"

"I gave him all my money and other valuables before I came up here," said de Priemo. "I asked him to keep it all for me but now I want it back."

This led Petrosino to surmise that Madonna, after collecting the funds, had been robbed and murdered, perhaps by Petto who had been seen spending money in a lavish way. Then he went to Buffalo to meet Madonna's widow. She identified the photograph as that of her husband and recognized the watch which had been pawned by Petto and later recovered by Petrosino. To guard against the remote possibility of error, she was brought to the New York morgue where she positively identified the body. The detective was ready now for legal action.

Petto was arrested on a charge of murder and seven of his associates were booked as accessories. However, when the case was called in court, most of the witnesses had disappeared in fear of Mafia violence and the few who did appear refused to testify. There was no alternative but to dismiss the case for lack of evidence.

Morello was then arrested on a charge of counterfeiting and sentenced to serve twenty years. Petto immediately left New York and settled in a small Pennsylvania town.

Years later, de Priemo, long after his release from prison, encountered Petrosino in an East Side wineshop and asked for "my old friend Petto." The detective made some inquiries and learned that Petto had long since been shot to death.

"I guess that closes the case after all," he said.

As cases of this type continued, Petrosino became increasingly concerned over the steady stream of Mafia gangsters arriving in New York. Though he was aware of their identity and their activities, he found it difficult if not impossible to charge them with crime for terrified victims feared to contact the authorities. The only course, he believed, lay in vigorous use of immigration laws to deport the newcomers as known criminals and undesirable aliens. This, however, was difficult to do since the law required that to establish grounds for deportation there must be proof of criminal activity within three years of residence in the United States.

Petrosino urged stricter interpretation of regulations. Support came from men of influence and from the press. Congress authorized the appointment of an Immigration Commission to study the problem, and, through the efforts of one of its members, Professor Jeremiah W. Jenks of Cornell University, a plan evolved. It called for the gathering of evidence in Italy and Sicily against Mafia criminals who already had come to America and those ready to emigrate, the latter to be turned back on arrival. This, it was believed, would greatly expedite the work of immigration officials in deporting terrorists.

The proposal was referred to the Police Department which agreed to send Petrosino to Italy for a lengthy stay to uncover the necessary evidence.

The trip, which began late in February 1909, was arranged with the utmost secrecy and only a few in the highest levels of police administration knew of his departure. With him he took credentials signed by Commissioner Bingham addressed to the chiefs of police of Italy. They announced, in part, that *"Petrosino is under orders to make investigations in Italy with reference to Italian criminals who are now in the United States or who may be planning to come to this country. Will appreciate any assistance you may be able to give him."*

He went first to Rome where he called on the Minister of the Interior, presenting his credentials and proudly displaying the gold watch that had been given him by the Italian consul. The Minister, Peano, became so interested that he instructed Francisco Leonardi, Director of Police for all of Italy, to issue orders denying passports to Italian criminals contemplating a visit to the United States.

Petrosino was offered police guards which he stubbornly refused, explaining with his usual air of confidence that such measures were wholly unnecessary, especially since his work would be veiled in secrecy. When he departed he took with him a letter signed by the Minister asking all police officers in Italy and Sicily for their fullest cooperation. In effect, Petrosino had the authority of a high-ranking Italian police official.

He went to Palmero in Sicily where he registered at the Hotel de France as Guglielmo de Simoni. Influenza kept him in bed for a week before he could begin his work—but fate was to intercede.

At nine o'clock on the night of March 12, walking through the Piazza Marina, he stopped to admire the Garibaldi statue. Moments later two men sneaked up from behind and four shots rang out. Two pierced his head; the others penetrated his lungs. From the ground Petrosino drew his revolver and fired two wild shots. An instant later he was dead. A Belgian revolver with one discharged chamber lay near the body.

News of the assassination created a furore throughout Europe and the United States. Diplomatic messages were exchanged and police throughout Europe were called on to round up Mafia suspects. The Italian Government offered a reward of 10,000 lira, a large sum in those days, for capture of the murderers. Similar offers came from New York police and private sources but the killers were never found nor was the plot ever uncovered.

Some believed that Petrosino had been followed by assassins from the United States. Others blamed a newspaper for its "scoop" revealing that the detective had gone to Sicily. Whatever the cause, all acknowledged that one of the greatest detectives of his day had fallen.

Tributes came from many in high places. President Theodore Roosevelt, who during the days when he was Police Commissioner of New York had known Petrosino well, cabled:

PETROSINO WAS A GREAT AND A GOOD MAN. I KNEW HIM FOR YEARS. HE DID NOT KNOW THE NAME OF FEAR AND WAS A MAN WORTH WHILE. I REGRET HIS DEATH MOST SINCERELY.

New York voted Petrosino's widow, Adelina, a pension of $1000 a year. On March 12, 1910, a monument to the martyred officer was unveiled in New York's Calvary Cemetery in the presence of members of his family, friends, and high police officials. It marked their last tribute to a fallen hero.

Chapter 9

Trapping Dynamiters

William J. Burns

For almost six years, from early in 1905 to late in 1910, sixteen states of the Union were caught in the grip of one of the most violent and costly labor wars in the nation's history. The closed shop was the issue. Dynamite and nitroglycerin were the weapons used by the aggressors.

Opposing forces were the International Union of Bridge and Structural Iron Workers, whose members were on strike, and the National Erectors Association, an employers' organization insisting on the right to hire both union and non-union workers.

The years of bitter warfare were marked by eighty-six explosions that destroyed railroad bridges, buildings and huge stockpiles of structural materials with losses mounting to many millions. Fiendishly designed time bombs were often used. Police officers and non-union workers were brutally assaulted; some fatally and others seriously injured.

Defying arrest, the terrorists gradually broadened the base of their campaign, extending it beyond the properties of the National Erectors to include other employers opposing organized labor. Then, suddenly, the battlefield moved far west to Los Angeles where on the morning of October 1, 1910, the building of the *Los Angeles Times* was blown up with a toll of twenty-one dead and scores seriously hurt. It was the penalty imposed on the owner, General Harrison

Gray Otis, for his prolonged and bitter fight against the unions.

Industrialists now were gripped with greater fear, not knowing when or where the next blow would come. Their only hope lay in the ability of a nationally-known detective who already had started on the trail of the dynamiters, a shrewd investigator who had demonstrated his mettle in numbers of difficult and complicated cases. He was William J. Burns, whose experience and methods qualified him to undertake this latest baffling case. But first, let us meet the man and learn something of his background.

In physique and dress Burns looked like a successful businessman. In a way, he was the antithesis of the story book detective. Stoutly built with a florid face and heavy blond mustache, he would be conspicuous in any crowd. His clothes were always well tailored and immaculately kept. He wore the hard black derby of the era and his double-breasted gold watch chain fitted perfectly into the ensemble.

He liked to relate his experiences and while those who listened sometimes perceived a lack of modesty, they always agreed that he had earned a right to gloat over his accomplishments and to display his flair for showmanship when he chose. Many called him "Never Fail Burns."

He often asserted that his success, like that in any business or profession, resulted from hard work, good judgment and sound thinking.

Many said that he was born to be a detective, although he spent his early years as a cutter for his father, who operated a fashionable men's tailoring shop in Columbus, Ohio. He might have continued in the business had not his father been elected a police commissioner in that city, which gave young William the opportunity to visit police stations and listen to the exploits of veterans in crime detection.

During this time he first played detective when he found his uniformed friends seriously perplexed by a series of burglaries. Whether by guess or clever deduction, he pointed an accusing finger at a certain man in the community then beyond suspicion. An arrest confirmed his judgment.

Not long afterward Columbus faced an election scandal when it was discovered that some three hundred votes in one precinct had been cast illegally. A citizens committee asked young Burns to investigate. In surprisingly short time he ascertained that a jailer had permitted a notorious safe-cracker to open the vault in which the tallies had been locked, after which a convicted forger, working within the jail, had altered the records in a forged handwriting of the tally sheet.

In 1888, soon after he had turned twenty-six, Burns was hired as a full-time investigator for a private detective agency in St. Louis but government service attracted him and he joined the Treasury Department as an operative. Later he transferred to the Secret Service where he remained for more than twenty years. He became the nemesis of counterfeiters.

One of his most valuable undercover men in this work was a former counterfeiter, Charlie Ulrich. After promising that he had reformed, Ulrich took his family to Germany but on his return Burns learned that he was again making plates for spurious currency.

To watch the man, Burns moved his family to Cincinnati where Ulrich was living and set them up in an apartment across the street from the suspect's home. After four months of close surveillance, aided by his wife, the detective confronted Ulrich with proof of his illegal operations. Then he played on the man's emotions, berating him for being a poor husband and father. Ulrich was so deeply moved that he agreed to become a secret agent. Burns always credited him with gathering the evidence that led to the capture of one of the most powerful counterfeiting rings in the country.

This was in a period when government agents were seriously worried by a wide circulation of bogus coin and currency. Late in 1897 Burns undertook to trace the makers of a worthless Monroe-head hundred dollar silver certificate in popular use at the time—a counterfeit bill so perfectly made that every government expert but one declared it to be genuine. The fraud had been detected by a shrewd Sub-Treasury teller in Philadelphia who found that the ink blurred when he lay a dampened finger on the note. The discovery frightened bankers throughout the country.

At the outset Burns realized that it would be necessary to contact every engraver capable of such meticulously perfect work. Months later the culprits were identified but not until a year later had he gathered sufficient evidence to convict the thirteen members of the ring. His feat won high commendation and Chief Wilkie of the Secret Service called him "the best man we have."

With such status he was "loaned" in 1904 to work with Francis J. Heney, a noted government lawyer, in cleaning up the Oregon land fraud cases which had become a national scandal. As a shrewd and resourceful detective, Burns delved into the operations of those carrying on a wholesale land swindle against the government and his evidence led to the indictment of more than one hundred individuals. A United States Senator was convicted and died while his appeal was pending; a federal district attorney fell into political oblivion.

Burns returned triumphantly to Washington not knowing that two years later he would be called back to the West for an equally if not more difficult task.

This was at a time when graft was rampant in San Francisco government and a fearless crusading newspaper editor, Fremont Older, was crying for reform. After securing the promise of a leading financier and civic leader of the community, Rudolph Spreckels, to support a clean-up campaign, Older took the problem to Washington and pleaded with President Theodore Roosevelt for assistance.

Heney and Burns, on the basis of their achievement in Oregon, were the logical men to be selected and the President arranged for their transfer to California. Burns arrived in late May of 1906, little more than a month after the disastrous earthquake and fire while much of the city lay in ruins.

He was informed that the municipal government was under the domination of Boss Ruef, that privileges were bought and paid for, and that certain members of the Board of Supervisors, the county legislative body, were taking bribes from utility corporations for franchises. Prostitution, gambling, and other forms of vice flourished under government protection.

Older, using his reporters as detectives, had scratched the surface but a man of Burns' caliber and experience was needed to produce concrete evidence. It did not take him long to evolve a plan of action.

At the time of his arrival in the city social workers were crusading against skating rinks, claiming that they were breeding places for vice. An ordinance aimed at closing them was before the supervisors and appeared to be certain of passage. This gave Burns an idea.

Working with the owner of the largest rink who agreed to serve the prosecution, Burns set a trap. Unwilling to trust a workman with his secret scheme, he borrowed a brace and bit from a friendly grocer near the rink and bored three little holes in the wall of the rink owner's private office. A supervisor was sent for and offered $500 if he would vote against the ordinance. With Burns' eye glued to the peephole, the city official accepted the bribe in marked currency. Two others, appearing in quick succession, did the same. Then the three trapped officials confessed all that they knew of city graft—and they had many startling facts to tell. In the end, Ruef went to prison and an honest administration was swept into office.

Burns again returned to Washington and soon resigned

to organize in 1909 the international detective agency that still bears his name. Since his death on April 14, 1932, at the age of seventy, it has operated under the direction of his sons, Raymond and Sherman.

The wave of dynamiting and other terror in the labor war that provided Burns with his most celebrated case actually had begun five years before he was called on to hunt the perpetrators and bring them to justice. The trail, extending over many states, was marked by a succession of clues which Burns followed personally with the aid of a small army of operatives. His investigation had been under way less than a month when the *Times* explosion occurred.

Industrialists and wealthy businessmen, who once had been concerned only over property losses, were now fearing for their lives. One of them, David M. Parry of Indianapolis, a past president of the National Association of Manufacturers, was moving about with a bodyguard after being hounded by threats of death. So determined were his enemies that they finally threatened to kidnap his children. In desperation, Parry sent them with his wife to Europe, where they remained until Burns had finished his work. Others were taking similar precautions.

Brutal assaults had become almost a daily occurrence. In New York a policeman was beaten on the roof of the Hotel Plaza, then under construction, and hurled unconscious to the pavement. On the following day acid was thrown in the face of a non-union steel worker.

It was on September 5, 1910, that Burns was summoned by the McClintic-Marshall Construction Company of Pittsburgh, one of the largest and most influential concerns in its field. A railroad bridge at Indiana Harbor in Indiana, built by this firm, had been blown up at 10:30 o'clock the previous night shortly before the approach of a passenger train. Almost at the same time an 80-ton steel girder prepared by the company to span the Illinois River for the

Pekin & Peoria Railroad in East Peoria had been blasted and hours later there were two explosions in the foundry of Lucas & Sons in Peoria, Illinois.

When Burns sat down with officials of the McClintic-Marshall concern they told him frankly that they doubted his ability to uncover the plot for they and their associates had previously engaged private agencies to augment the work of local and state police, but all efforts had failed.

He was informed that in each case nitroglycerin had been used and that no evidence of any value had been left behind. "Have you any theory, any explanation that might help me at the start?" Burns inquired.

"Only that we are running an open shop and intend to continue doing so," he was informed.

"In that case," the detective reasoned, "isn't it likely that the Bridge and Structural Iron Workers Union would be a good place for me to begin my work?"

"Could be—but you're the detective. Do whatever you think is best for the most promising results."

Pressing the others further, he was informed that only days before John J. McNamara, secretary and treasurer of the Union; and H. S. Hockins, its professional organizer, had called on the company to demand that it change its policy and hire only Union men. The reply was a blunt refusal and through channels of its own the concern learned that its property would be blown up. Precautions obviously were ineffective.

"How widespread has been this destruction?" Burns inquired.

He was told that the Pittsburgh Construction Company had suffered heavy losses in Newark and Cleveland, that equipment of the American Bridge Company in Cleveland had been blasted, and that a mill in Conshohocken, Pennsylvania had been burned—but these were only a few examples of the terror reign that readily came to mind. In

1908, for example, there had been twenty costly explosions in various states.

Burns began by visiting the scene where nitroglycerin had been set under the huge girder of the McClintic-Marshall Company. He found that another charge had been placed under another girder of similar size but had failed because of a defective dry battery connected to a clock-work bomb which could be left nearly twelve hours before an explosion would occur, giving the culprits more than ample time to escape. Similar devices, he already knew, had been used to set off most of the explosions. They were simply but ingeniously made—a cheap alarm clock fastened to a battery with wires leading to a ten-quart can of nitroglycerin.

After putting the unexploded time bomb aside for more careful study, Burns turned his attention to a large tin containing the explosive which remained intact. It bore a mark "X Cummy McFarland & Co.—Open Hearth." A distance away lay a box of sawdust in which the two cans apparently had been packed for safety. The wooden box had been made from two smaller ones, their ends knocked out with the sides held together by cleats. One was marked "NEO black," the other "NEO purple," indicating that they had contained either ink or paint.

Burns now had his first clues, though he feared that the clock, of the common, cheap type used in many homes, might be impossible to trace. However, he was confident that the sawdust would prove a valuable lead and he put some of it carefully into a paper bag. Then he turned his attention to the nitroglycerin, knowing that since it cannot be transported on trains, it usually is moved only over short distances because of danger in handling.

Suspecting that in this case it had been moved by horse and buggy, he began by inquiring at livery stables over a wide area. Operatives who had joined him visited numerous hotels and lodging houses where the dynamiters might have stayed. Their search finally led to M. J. Morehart of Portland, Indiana, an agent for the Independent Torpedo Company, who recognized the nitroglycerin can as his.

Morehart remembered that on August 20 a stranger introducing himself as J. W. McGraw had called on him asking the price of nitroglycerin in large quantities. He said that he represented George Clark & Company of Indianapolis, who operated a quarry and needed the explosive to blast unusually hard rock.

Nine days later McGraw had telephoned to Morehart from Muncie, Indiana, ordering one hundred quarts of nitroglycerin. A meeting place was arranged on a highway outside of Albany, Indiana, since the law did not permit such a delivery within city limits.

The men had met as planned, McGraw coming in a light delivery wagon containing boxes, a shovel and a quantity of sawdust. Morehart helped McGraw transfer ten tins into the boxes and the two had carefully placed sawdust around the cans. From a bulging roll of bills, McGraw had paid the other $130 after stating that he intended driving to Muncie where his purchase would be transferred to an automobile and taken to Peoria. That was the last that Morehart had ever seen of his customer.

Burns and his men, now having a good description of McGraw, moved to Muncie where they learned that he had registered at a local hotel. His signature was carefully traced should handwriting comparisons prove necessary later. They also located the stable where McGraw had rented the rig and a farm yard from which the sawdust had been stolen. A small quantity of it still remained in the wagon. Burns examined it closely with the aid of a strong lens, then compared it with that found close to the scene of the East Peoria explosion. The two samples, unusually coarse, were identical. They also matched sawdust dropped on the road outside of Albany where McGraw had received the explosives.

Further inquiries in Muncie disclosed that McGraw had

been joined there by a stranger in an automobile. They were traced to the Illinois River and there the trail ended abruptly.

The Clark concern mentioned by McGraw as his employer next drew Burns' attention. He went to Indianapolis and though he soon learned that no such firm existed, a significant thought went flashing through his mind. Why had the man chosen Indianapolis for the location of his mythical company? Was this city not the headquarters of the Bridge and Structural Iron Workers Union already under suspicion? Burns decided to look for an answer.

He soon picked up the trail of a man closely resembling McGraw who had been seen about Indianapolis with an unidentified companion. The two had been overheard talking about John J. McNamara, who previously had threatened the McClintic-Marshall Company.

Three weeks of intensive work now had passed since Burns had undertaken the case and he sat down with his men in his hotel room to review results. Little handfuls of sawdust had definitely linked McGraw to at least one of the explosions and there appeared to be no doubt but that their elusive suspect was heavily involved in the wave of destruction. His mention of Indianapolis still was regarded as vitally significant—but where was McGraw now? He had told Morehart that he would return for more purchases of nitroglycerin and the dealer had promised to notify the detective agency at once if he appeared. Burns frowned at the thought of waiting indefinitely though at the time he could not anticipate the shocking crime that would be perpetrated only days later.

It occurred far away, in Los Angeles, at one o'clock of the morning of October 1 in the plant of the *Times* while scores of men were busily at work on the day's editions. A terrific explosion in an alley behind the building had blown up an entire wall. Floors, heavily weighted with machinery, collapsed like tinderwood and flames soon roared through the wreckage. Some were hopelessly trapped; others leaped from windows. The structure became an inferno of indescribable horror.

When the fire was finally extinguished, twenty-one bodies, some of Union workers, were taken from the wreckage. Many others were seriously hurt. But the dynamiters had undertaken even more havoc.

While the ruins were being searched for victims and the police were holding back crowds of hysterical men and women, relatives of the trapped workers, a bomb in a suitcase was found in the basement of the home of General Otis, owner of the paper. It was moved hurriedly to an open area and exploded where it did little damage.

Minutes later a third bomb was found near the home of the secretary of the Los Angeles Merchants and Manu-facturers Association but police succeeded in disconnecting it in time to avert further loss of life. Los Angeles was gripped with terror.

At the time Burns was on his way to the western city to attend a meeting of one of his largest clients, the Ameri-can Bankers Association. In his absence his ablest men were trying to pick up the trail of McGraw.

The detective had not been in the panic-stricken city long before he received a call from its mayor, George B. Alexander, asking him to assume charge of the *Times* case. He already had linked it to the other explosions on which he had been working and he naturally accepted the assignment. In fact, Burns promptly gave the mayor the names of the men he believed responsible but the city's chief executive listened incredulously.

From his earlier study of the national labor scene, Burns knew that the organized iron workers in Los Angeles were on strike, pitting themselves against the powerful Merchants and Manufacturers organization whose fight for the open shop was strongly supported by Otis in his newspaper. In fact, anti-union sentiment was strong throughout the community, a sharp contrast from San Francisco then under a powerful union labor administration.

When Burns inquired about the *Times* explosion, he was told that nitroglycerin had been used just as in the other blasts. The clock devices in the two abortive bombings were identical with those he had found elsewhere.

Burns telegraphed for two of his men who had worked in the Peoria area to join him at once and he set to work. Obviously, finding the source of the explosives used to blow up the *Times* and the materials in the bombing attempts would be his first task.

The battery attached to the bomb left at the home of the Merchants and Manufacturers secretary was marked with a large letter "L." Days later it was traced to the store where it had been sold and a good description of the buyer was obtained, though his name was not known.

Explosives recovered from the attempted bombings led Burns to believe that they had come from the San Francisco area where the Giant Powder Company did a large business. He went north and soon discovered that he was being shadowed by men hired by the labor forces. In many instances he was obliged to move by circuitous routes to evade his pursuers.

His visit to the headquarters of the Giant Company was fruitful. Bruce McCall, a salesman, recalled that less than a month before, in the afternoon of September 15, he had received a telephone call from a man who said he represented the Bryson Construction Company of Sacramento and needed a quantity of high-powered dynamite to blow up tree stumps.

On the following day this man called at the office and was disappointed when McCall told him that this type of dynamite was not available but would be prepared especially for him and made available at the company's plant in the little town of Giant, across the bay from San Francisco. The customer paid $82.10 in advance and talked loquaciously about his troubles with tree stumps.

He had given his name as J. B. Bryson and was described by McCall and his associates as about thirty-two years of age, tall and smooth-shaven with a sandy complexion. All agreed that they could recognize him if he called again. "We didn't like his looks," McCall remarked. "He just wouldn't look you in the eye."

Six days later Bryson had returned with another man, a few years older but of similar build, and arranged for another purchase of the same material which they said would be taken to Auburn by launch. At this point McCall and one of his superiors, Thomas Branson, became suspicious and, thinking that the men perhaps were planning a train holdup, notified the authorities.

That afternoon McCall had received a telephone call from a third man who said his name was Leonard and that he would pick up the order placed by the other two. The salesman, now even more dubious and curious about the launch, replied that he would take the dynamite to the boat, but Leonard said that it was moored elsewhere and would be brought to the place of delivery by an associate.

An hour later still another man appeared, speaking with a Spanish accent. He gave his name as Morris and said that he would go to Oakland for the launch which was named the *Peerless*. He returned with the boat in a short time—much too short for a trip to Oakland—and delivery was made.

It was now for Burns to pick up the trail of the four mysterious men; to ascertain their movements in and about the launch. People who had seen them before and after obtaining the dynamite were interviewed and a number of interesting facts came to light. The craft had been renamed the *Pastime* and its various cruises from place to place were traced. From other sources it was learned that the men had rented an old house in an outlying part of San Francisco and when the investigators searched it they found ten cases of dynamite, two already opened and eight sewed up in burlap. All of it was covered with a heavy tarpaulin. However, there was no trace of the men.

The owner of the property informed the investigators that he had rented it to one William Capp, whose description tallied with that of Morris, one of the men to whom the dynamite had been delivered. The tarpaulin bore the name of the maker and when he was located he said that he had left it at an address on Grove Street where a family named Caplan had lived shortly before the *Times* explosion and left immediately after. Burns was certain that the tenant was David Caplan, an anarchist, whose wife was related to Emma Goldman, then one of the best known anarchists in the country.

Through other sources Burns ascertained that the man giving the name of Leonard was Matt A. Schmidt, known to his friends as "Schmitty," and also believed to be an anarchist.

The three had covered their trail and the detectives, despite intensive effort, were unable to obtain the slightest clue to their whereabouts; nor was there anything to indicate that the elusive McGraw, already implicated in the eastern explosions, was involved with them. Burns decided to go elsewhere to look for the suspects in the *Times* disaster and his son, Raymond, was left in charge of the investigation in the San Francisco area.

Burns, working on the "birds of a feather" theory, turned northward to Tacoma, Washington, where a small colony of anarchists lived in seclusion. It was likely, he reasoned, that Caplan, Bryson, and Schmidt were taking refuge there.

In a short time he located J. D. Waggoner, a trade school teacher, who remembered that a man named J. B. Bryson had called on him for instruction in using explosives and he had exhibited a time bomb similar to those used by the dynamiters. He also had with him a can containing dynamite with markings indicating that it had come from Portland, Indiana—the same place where McGraw had bought explosives for use in Peoria.

This, with evidence previously acquired, further supported Burns' theory that all of the dynamitings in widely separated areas were directed from a central location and by the same people. He still believed that headquarters were in Indianapolis and his men in that city were kept busy.

It was while Burns was slipping in and out of the anarchist colony, contacting his men who were searching for the suspects, that unexpected complications developed. Certain political forces in Los Angeles supporting organized labor had protested the payment of fees and expense money to Burns. He was bluntly informed that financing would stop unless he agreed to make daily progress reports and this, he was certain, would thwart his work. Rather than abandon the case, he chose to pay all expenses from his own pocket, a serious handicap in so extensive an investigation.

The detective turned again to Indianapolis where informants told him that a man resembling McGraw had been seen conversing with John J. McNamara. Not long afterward, Burns met McGraw face to face though the suspect was unaware of his pursuer's identity. Operatives were assigned at once to shadow McGraw day and night. He was finally followed to his home in Chicago and it was learned for the first time that his true name was Ortie McManigal, who later proved to be one of the key figures in the wholesale dynamiting plot.

Weeks later McManigal was trailed by Burns' men to the railroad station where he boarded a train to Kenosha, Wisconsin. There he was greeted by a friend with guns and other hunting equipment. They awaited a train from Chicago and when it arrived several others, similarly equipped, joined the pair. It seemed apparent that some of the dynamiters were planning to camp in the woods until the heat of the investigation would subside.

The party bought railroad tickets to Canover, Wisconsin, and while one Burns operative traveled with them on the same train, his partner remained behind to send for reinforcements.

Burns' men had no trouble in locating the camp of the hunters. Being seasoned undercovermen, they pitched their tents only a short distance away and soon detectives and their quarry were on a first name basis. One of McManigal's companions, known as Sullivan, became especially friendly with a Burns man, so friendly, in fact, that Sullivan agreed to let the detective snap his picture as a souvenir of their happy jaunt together. This, with a specimen of Sullivan's handwriting, was rushed to the nearest Burns office. Sullivan, it developed, was none other than J. B. Bryson, who had purchased the dynamite that blew up the *Times*.

The hunters broke camp more than a week later and in friendly parting the Burns men not only learned the destination of each man but succeeded in trailing them back to their homes. Sullivan, now revealed as Bryson, was shadowed to McManigal's residence in Chicago.

Questions of timing and strategy now confronted Burns. He believed that he had sufficient evidence to warrant Bryson's arrest but he still wanted first to firmly link the man with higher-ups. But since Bryson could easily be kept under surveillance day and night, there seemed to be no reason to jeopardize the main objective.

A day after the meeting of Bryson and McManigal in the latter's home, the two left together and were followed to a train bound for Indianapolis. Bryson went on, presumably for orders, but McManigal jumped off as the train was pulling out, apparently apprehensive. Each man, however, was shadowed.

In Indianapolis Bryson, obviously fearful that he was being trailed, zigzagged through the city, walking through several hotels until he finally settled in one and registered under the name of Sullivan. Early the next morning, still followed, he went by train to Cincinnati where he was met at the depot by a smooth-shaven stranger carrying heavy packages, which the detectives assumed contained explosives. Dogging behind the stranger was a Burns detective who had followed him from Indianapolis.

The two were trailed into a sparsely settled suburb to the home of Mrs. Mary T. McNamara, mother of John J., the Union's secretary-treasurer, and his brother, James B. But by this time Burns and his operatives had learned the true identity of the pair—Bryson was none other than James B. McNamara and the stranger was his brother, John J.

Around these two men Burns had woven a tight net of direct evidence. James B. McNamara, alias Bryson, had been identified as the buyer of the dynamite used in the *Times* explosion; McManigal, alias McGraw, had been unmasked as the man who purchased nitroglycerin at Portland, Indiana to blast the McClintic-Marshall girders at East Peoria. Direct evidence against John J. McNamara and his associates in the Union, regarded by Burns as the brains of the terror reign, still was lacking.

John J. was kept under constant surveillance as were his brother and McManigal. Months slipped by and Burns was running out of funds. He realized now that unless arrests were made without further delay it would be impossible to collect from the Los Angeles authorities. Under these circumstances, he decided to take McManigal and James B. McNamara into custody, gambling on his ability to wring a confession from one or the other.

The arrests took place in the lobby of the Oxford Hotel in Detroit on the morning of April 12, 1911. Neither man resisted but when informed that they were wanted for blowing open a safe they denied their guilt, boasting that they would be free in a short time. Their suitcases were filled with clocks, batteries and other bomb-making equipment.

Both men were taken to Chicago and on the way their

captors were offered bribes that finally amounted to $30,000 in return for their release. McManigal already was showing signs of nervousness and from his talk it was apparent that he feared he would be made a scapegoat for the others; that James McNamara would be quickly freed through the influence of his brother.

In Chicago Burns worked fast and with utmost secrecy to extradite the prisoners to Los Angeles. Publicity, he was aware, would put John J. McNamara on his guard and would mobilize the labor forces in defense of the accused. However, by rushing coded messages to his California offices, he was able to obtain secret warrants against the two prisoners and John J. McNamara.

Burns then called on McManigal who was being held under guard in the home of a police sergeant and related all that he had uncovered linking the prisoner with the dynamitings. He was told that if he chose to confess to clear his conscience he must do so without any promise of clemency. The detective further informed him of his legal rights and then withdrew, suggesting that he would be available if summoned.

The call came sooner than expected—in less than an hour. As Burns sat with McManigal in a closed room, the accused man related in startling detail his part in the widespread explosions. He implicated John J. McNamara and other high officials of the International Union in numerous dynamitings as well as the *Times* outrage. It was a dramatic climax to long months of work by Burns and his men.

There now was no longer reason for delaying the arrest of John J. McNamara. Burns hastened to Indianapolis, showed his telegraphic warrant to police officials who accompanied him to Union headquarters. They found McNamara in conference with other officers of his organization and told him that he was under arrest. Taken completely by surprise, he scanned the warrant and readily consented to accompany the officers to the station.

Burns still had other important work to do. With police assigned to help him, he drove to the farm of a man named Jones in the outskirts of Indianapolis where McManigal had said a large cache of explosives was kept by John J. McNamara in a piano box.

Jones met the party, unaware of their purpose, and led them to a huge box in the barn. "Who does that belong to?" Burns inquired.

"To J. J. McNamara," the farmer answered. "He keeps old books in there—old records of the Union, you know."

The detective unlocked the box with a key taken from James McNamara. It was filled with dynamite and nitroglycerin.

The group then went to Union headquarters with a search warrant for examination of the vault. It contained ninety-two pounds of dynamite, fourteen alarm clocks and a mass of correspondence addressed to the Union secretary relating to "jobs" to be done in various parts of the country.

It became necessary now to check every essential detail in McManigal's confession, a task that called for the services of investigators in many states. They received their orders from Burns Agency offices in key cities and as they moved about they uncovered still more explosives and bomb materials stored in the most unexpected places. Everything of importance that McManigal had said was finally verified.

Meanwhile, in Los Angeles, arrangements were progressing for the trials of the three accused men and Burns was kept busy guarding against attempts to intimidate important witnesses and prospective jurors. Once he learned that an influential Western leader among the iron workers was endeavoring to "plant" a spy in the prosecution ranks. Burns adroitly obliged him—the spy was one of the detective's undercovermen. But other unexpected troubles developed.

From supporters of the accused men there came a hue

and cry against Burns. He was accused of kidnapping the defendants and, despite the absurdity of the charge, he was indicted by the grand jury in Indianapolis for abducting John J. McNamara. The charge was eventually dropped.

Defense forces were busy in other ways. A huge defense fund was raised to obtain able counsel and Clarence Darrow, recognized as the foremost lawyer in his field, was engaged to represent the accused. His confidence of acquittal was suddenly shattered on December 1, 1911, when the two McNamara brothers appeared in court and admitted their guilt. James B., pleading guilty to the *Times* dynamiting and the twenty-one deaths resulting, was sentenced to serve the remainder of his life in San Quentin Penitentiary. His brother, entering a similar plea of guilt in the dynamiting of the Llewellyn Iron Works in Los Angeles, shortly after the *Times* bombing, was sent to the same prison for fifteen years. McManigal, as a reward for his confession and great assistance to the prosecution, received immunity.

Darrow, greatly chagrined, admitted that so far as the defense was concerned, "there never was a chance to win."

With the two McNamaras in prison, Burns moved to Indianapolis taking McManigal with him. The latter's exposure of all that he knew and of his own activities, coupled with the evidence that Burns had accumulated, resulted in the arrest of forty-five officials of the International Union. Thirty-eight of them were convicted and sent to prison for terms ranging from one to seven years.

Leadership of the Structural Iron Workers Union passed into the hands of honest, dedicated men and Burns turned to other cases entrusted to his international agency.

Chapter 10

A Game of Cat and Mouse

Charles Chenevier

Throughout France, Charles Chenevier is regarded as one
of his country's most skillful detectives, an extraordinary
man with methods and philosophy all his own. Though he
retired from public service in 1957 with the honorary title
of Assistant Director of the Sureté Nationale, an organization similar in many respects to the FBI or Scotland
Yard, he still follows his profession as a private investigator.

Despite his vigorous career which began in 1925, he
has lost none of his enthusiasm or his energy. Four inches
under six feet in height, he is heavy-set and his thick
black hair shows no sign of gray. His voice is low, with
a slight remnant of his Southern accent and when he
speaks he gestures freely to emphasize his words, while
his black eyes stare into the face of his listener.

Of his many tributes and awards he is proudest of his
decoration as a Commander of the Legion of Honor, a reward for his work in the French underground which
finally led to months of torture in a German prison camp.
It was the price he paid for his loyalty to his native France.

At the time of the German occupation he had been stationed in Vichy, the seat of the Marshal Pétain government.
There he came upon information which he was certain
would be of vital concern to the retreating French officials
and with difficulty he smuggled it to the French military
counter-spy service in London. Before long, rumors of his

activity reached the Gestapo and he was closely watched, yet he might have avoided trouble had not another police officer, one of his friends, been arrested by the Nazis for similar aid to France. In the prisoner's pocket the Germans found a list of people active in the resistance. Chenevier's name was among them. He was arrested November 11, 1943, and deported to a camp in Neueugamm, Germany, popularly called "Slow Death." There he remained until Germany fell.

Pursuing criminals, Chenevier still maintains, is like playing poker. "In poker," he explains, "a player must hide his own strength from his adversary, at the same time forcing his opponent to uncover his strength."

Unlike many of his contemporaries, he does not hesitate to admit that he has always worked with "stool pigeons"; in fact, he insists that a successful police officer must always look to them for assistance. "Informers," he often says, "constitute a type of beast which must be cultivated in the criminal jungle. I always told my inspectors: 'If you have no informers you had better find another trade in which you will do better than in police work.'"

Chenevier, nevertheless, fully recognizes the hazard in such relations. "It is necessary to hold informers without letting them hold you," he cautions. "They are often deceitful and sometimes difficult to control. It is necessary, however, to count more on them than on the magnifying glass of Sherlock Holmes or upon the deductions of an Edgar Allan Poe, but an officer should never take their word as gospel. They often lie or exaggerate for their own selfish ends. One must be on his guard but, for myself, being neither divine nor a prophet, I always managed to keep a few 'stool-pigeons' on hand."

He holds as firmly to other beliefs, like his theory that a confession should not be a detective's major goal. To the contrary, he contends, an efficient officer, before making an arrest, should develop evidence so conclusive that an admission of guilt is only a formal but unnecessary sequence. "I have always claimed," Chenevier argues, "that once located and identified, a gangster must be left to himself— at liberty—but closely watched. His every act and movement must be observed so that when the arrest is finally made at the desired moment his past has been examined under the microscope and the prisoner is astonished to find an officer who needs to ask only a very few questions. In that case it is easy to proceed without a confession; why get one since already a file of irrefutable proof of the man's guilt has been accumulated. His questioning is useful only in so far as it may clear up minor details. Such a method demands perseverance and patience; it involves risks, and the officer's skill is put to severe test for one false move can nullify the efforts of many months."

Chenevier always admonished his men to act calmly and with deliberation; to meticulously prepare every detail of a case to establish proof of guilt. "Witnesses and their testimony must be carefully assembled," he says, "and the facts must be irrefutable, for the man who has confessed his guilt today may repudiate it the next."

He contends that the super-policeman exists only in crime fiction; that officers in real life are subject to human error which should be kept at its lowest possible minimum. "Never hurry," he often told his men. "In your haste you can make mistakes; to act too fast may deprive you of your trump card—surprise. An arrest should be made without resistance. Always remember that a gangster, as terrible as he may be, will be powerless to draw his weapons if you plan his capture carefully in advance—if you arrange to take him by surprise."

As a small boy in his native town of Montelimar in the Rhone Valley near Avignon, where he was born November 2, 1901, young Chenevier amused himself by playing cops and robbers. While his companions took the parts of glorified gangsters, Charles saw himself always as the victorious policeman dedicated to law enforcement. It was a role that could not be attributed to atavism, for his father was a career officer in the Army.

He was still playing gang war games when an incident served to strengthen his desire for a police career. In a cafe near his home, the boy had witnessed the fatal shooting of a courageous police officer by the bandit he had just arrested. Then and there, Charles Chenevier resolved more firmly than before that he would devote his life to chasing criminals.

Circumstances, however, turned his ambitions into another field but not for long. He had just finished his secondary studies after his father's death on the Verdun battlefield when he was introduced to Ernest Lavisse, the noted historian of l'Académie Française, who believed that the young man should be a journalist. Through Lavisse's efforts, Chenevier became a newspaper reporter but after several years he gave up the work, choosing instead to follow his original plans.

It was 1925 and the authorities of France, harassed by an increasing number of murders and other serious crimes, organized a special corps of inspectors to cope with the situation. At twenty-four, Charles Chenevier applied for a place in the new organization. He was accepted and started at the bottom of the ladder.

His first experience, probably the easiest in his long career, served to encourage his yearning to become a great detective. A raw recruit, he was on night duty in the Saint-Lazare Station when an Englishman reported the theft of his topcoat on an incoming train. "Wait here for a while," the young officer told him. "I'll see what I can do."

Two hours later Chenevier returned with the coat on his arm. He had simply visited bars where known thieves congregated and the stolen garment was easily recovered. "You are better than Scotland Yard," the grateful traveler told him. Chenevier resolved then and there that he would justify the tribute but two years of dull, uninteresting desk work lay ahead. He spent them in a station near the Belgian border inspecting passports and customs papers; then for a time he was assigned to the archives service, simply filing the records of criminals that he yearned to capture.

The opportunity for which he had waited so patiently did not come until May 16, 1928, when he was assigned to a mobile brigade of judiciary police, a corps of specialists who, under the Sureté, have jurisdiction over criminal investigations throughout France. He had been selected at the request of Commissionaire Jean Belin, then recognized as one of the top men of the entire Sureté. Belin already had seen in the young officer a man of rare ability and resourcefulness.

On his first assignment in his new capacity, Chenevier justified the confidence of his sponsor by quickly solving the mysterious murder of an elderly man in his home in Raincy, a Paris suburb. By neighbors he was told that the victim was an affluent "rentier," one who lives on the income of his properties. This naturally suggested robbery as a motive. Checking further, Chenevier learned the name of a strange character who had been loitering for days about the house where the killing occurred—a man with no known occupation who slept wherever he could find shelter.

"Such a person," Chenevier explained later, "probably would not get far from the scene. The woods near the dead man's home would be a logical place for him to hide—and I played in luck."

Calling on the military for help, the detective surrounded the woods and found the wanted man in an abandoned cabin. He did not resist and soon admitted his guilt.

For the next six years Chenevier was engaged in a succession of important cases. Further recognition came to him in 1934 when Belin was advanced to the rank of Chef de Service with general control of research for the Sureté and he chose his young friend to be one of the top members of his team, a relationship that continued even after Chenevier had risen to the rank of commissionaire, a post comparable to superintendent or captain of detectives.

At about this time Chenevier gradually came into the limelight as a major figure in two sensational cases that shook all of France and ultimately gave him front page attention. The first of these is still known as "the Prince Affair," a mystery of death that followed in the wake of the Stavinsky scandal which led to sweeping governmental changes.

The scandal, a monumental swindle, involved the get-rich-quick operations of a forty-six-year-old Russian, Alexandre Stavinsky, also known as Serge Alexandre, who had fraudulently used the municipal loan office—commonly called "the mont-de piété"—at Bayonne in southwest France to carry on his nefarious fraud. The dénouement came in December 1933 with the arrest of the institution's cashier and only then did the full impact of Stavinsky's daring scheme fall on a startled nation. He had been lending money on jewels which he then pawned at the "mont-de-piété" to obtain funds for himself. His transactions, fast pyramiding, involved more than 100 million francs in losses to his victims who, clamoring for return of their valuables, turned to the police for help.

Stavinsky had been forewarned and when officers reached his office, he had vanished. Early in January 1934 he was traced to the Swiss frontier and police, led by Commissionaire Carpenter, surrounded his cottage. As Carpenter entered he heard a shot. Stavinsky was dead, apparently a suicide.

The rightist press, however, insisted that he had been assassinated by police to protect influential politicians implicated in the fraud, a claim still heard today whenever the case is mentioned.

Inflaming articles in *L'Action Française*, the royalists' publication, led to bloody rioting on February 6, 1934, when many were killed and hundreds wounded in fierce clashes between rival demonstrators.

France was still seething with excitement when the Prince Affair came as a shocking sequel with Chenevier destined to play an important part. Albert Prince, a state's attorney attached to the Paris Appeal Court, had been assigned to study two earlier police reports revealing Stavinsky's previous activities as a swindler, since many insisted that the police, long cognizant of his past, should have prevented his later operations.

On a day when Prince was due to testify before a Parliamentary Commission, his body was found on the railroad tracks near Dijon, leading some of the investigators to believe that he had been struck by a locomotive, a conclusion doubted by others who were puzzled by the finding of a large hunting knife on the ground near the corpse.

The news was reported to the waiting commissioners by the Minister of Justice and the Minister of the Interior, who announced that Prince had been murdered by the Mafia and that his assassins already were surrounded.

Again the opposition press cried scandal, boldly charging that the Minister of the Interior, virtually chief of all police in France, had hired a killer to silence Prince for the protection of a high government official who was said to have been one of Stavinsky's accomplices.

Though more conservative elements hinted at suicide, the murder accusations created a furore that divided people into rival factions. No one doubted that Prince's death would save the honor of certain high officials in the Palace of Justice, yet there appeared to be no evidence of murder. Bizarre developments added to the turmoil.

A police inspector of dubious integrity suddenly announced with an air of triumph that he had arrested three assassins. They were freed twenty-four hours later, a trio of nondescript beggars. The officer, incidentally, was shot after the liberation of France for collaboration with the Gestapo.

Soon afterward, a celebrated clairvoyant came forward claiming definite knowledge of Prince's assassination.

There were tragic repercussions resulting from mysterious and sinister political entanglements that have never been fully explained.

One high official in the state attorney's office took poison, a staff member of the Ministry of Agriculture cut his throat, a noted attorney leaped into the Seine, and the state's attorney dropped dead.

At the height of this excitement, the Ministry of the Interior assigned Commissionaire Chenevier to delve deeply into the case in the hope that rumor and dissension might be ended.

Chenevier's arrival in Dijon to begin his work aroused the anger of the district attorney who told him bluntly that he had not asked for help and did not need it. Ignoring this official, the detective began by tracing Prince's movements, almost minute by minute, for twenty-four hours preceding his death. Then, reconstructing the tragedy, he found that Prince had been struck from behind as he knelt between the rails. The front of the locomotive bore evidence of the impact.

The hunting knife, found close to the body, was traced to its seller, though a manufacturer's mark had been mysteriously obliterated with a file. Prince was identified as the buyer. There were other significant facts.

When the long inquiry was over, Chenevier was convinced that Prince had died a suicide, victim of "a guilty conscience." This conclusion was based on a number of vital findings, particularly the character of Prince's private life, his financial ruin, and his obvious negligence in the Stavinsky case.

Despite continuing controversy, pressed mostly by royalists, Chenevier's report was recognized as evidence of his thoroughness and, above all, his "incorruptibility." Modestly, he insisted that his work was only routine. "I merely started with the knife found by the body," he remarked, "and worked back, step by step and day by day, looking into Prince's private life."

The second of the two sensational cases was of a widely different nature. It involved the holdup of the Aga Khan and his French wife as they were driven by their chauffeur through the gates of their palatial Mediterranean villa, Yakimour, near Cannes. The robbery evidently had been carefully planned and was methodically carried out.

Covered by the revolvers of three men, the Aga Khan handed over a valise containing jewels valued at 200 million francs and 250,000 francs in currency. Included was a famous diamond known in France as La Marquise, worth 60 million francs and the favorite gem of the Aga Khan's wife, familiarly called La Begum.

The police rounded up near Cannes a gang of Corsicans suspected of complicity but the arrests yielded no trace of the stolen jewels. Five months later Commissionaire Truchi of Marseilles received a mysterious telephone call, an unidentified voice telling him to look for a package in the courtyard of the police building. In the parcel were all of the stolen gems—except La Marquise. Its recovery obviously was a task that called for the skill and intuition that only Chenevier could provide.

First, as usual, he put his informers to work and before long he learned that a Corsican named Mathieu, who ran a bar near the Champs Elysées, owned a diamond that resembled La Marquise. Chenevier secretly entered and searched Mathieu's rooms but the diamond could not be found. He did, however, find instruments of the sort used to measure and weigh precious stones. Mathieu, confronted by the detective, denied all knowledge of the theft.

Convinced of Mathieu's connection with the robbery but unable to hold him, Chenevier had him trailed day and night. Bits of information established that the suspect actually had been in possession of the jewel, which he had bought in Marseilles and turned over to a notorious character known as "Maurice les Cheveaux Blancs" to be recut. Subsequently, the diamond had been offered to a rich American but negotiations for the sale had stopped abruptly when Mathieu became aware that he was being watched by the police.

Chenevier faced a challenging problem. Though he now knew who had the jewel, he realized that recovering it would call for ingenious strategy. He proceeded to develop a daring ruse. An old friend, a highly trusted jewelry salesman, agreed to act as intermediary in a plan that was to cost the detective sleepless nights of worry over the risk of losing a costly set of borrowed diamonds to be used in his scheme.

Under the plan that was evolved, the salesman contacted Mathieu and told him that the efforts to sell La Marquise had become known even in legitimate channels and that he, the salesman, had a customer willing to pay far more for the diamond than the first prospect's offer. Mathieu cautiously took the bait and warily demanded some convincing guarantee of the salesman's reliability. Chenevier induced an insurance company to lend him a set of diamonds worth 25 million francs. These the salesman trustingly turned over to Mathieu, who readily recognized their value and sent word to his accomplice, Maurice, to return La Marquise to him.

Advised of this move by his intermediary, Chenevier took up a vigil near Maurice's quarters, prepared to arrest him when he emerged with the costly gem. As Maurice stepped out, the detective seized him and demanded the diamond. The startled man glared at the officer and indignantly declared: "I don't know what you're talking about."

For tense moments Chenevier feared that Maurice had sensed the trap and hidden the gem, while Mathieu meanwhile had absconded with the borrowed stones. Brushing aside this momentary doubt, Chenevier backed Maurice into a doorway and minutely searched his clothing. The diamond was found sewed into the lining of a vest pocket. With Maurice safely in jail, Chenevier hastened to Mathieu's home, arrested him, and retrieved the borrowed gems.

The case which won for Chenevier his greatest fame throughout all of France involved his long and successful pursuit of the country's Public Enemy No. 1—Emile Buisson, better known to the police as Mimile. Desperate and elusive, he was wanted for fully ten murders and more than eighty armed robberies which had netted him at least sixty million francs during his reign of terror. After three escapes from jails, the police had dubbed him "L'Insaissable," the uncapturable or the unseizable.

During the earlier years of Buisson's criminal activities Chenevier occasionally had been called on to assist in apprehending him, especially as the man gradually became more desperate and cunning. It was Chenevier who singlehanded and by a clever ruse finally recaptured him after his escapes from custody.

By the beginning of 1947 Buisson had assumed the leadership of a gang of gunmen who were terrorizing the country despite the most vigorous efforts of the police to trap him. It was during this later period, when Buisson's criminal career had reached its peak, that Chenevier was put in full charge of the case, with orders to capture France's most wanted man.

He already knew much of Buisson's past and of its origin. One of ten children, Emile was the son of an alcoholic chimney sweep and a mother who died insane. By his father the boy was taught to steal his food. At nine he was first arrested for thievery in a store in Lyon. For this he served a short term in a reformatory and soon resumed his evil ways.

A brother, Jean Baptiste, nicknamed "Le Nus," was an eager partner. As children, the two had pledged themselves to help each other out of trouble. The alliance was to continue through the years, even to prison breaks.

In 1947, when Chenevier personally undertook to end Buisson's wave of crime, the fugitive was forty-five, small and stocky. In no way did he look like a gangster. Suiting dress and manner to the needs of an intended crime, he would appear variously as a hard-working laborer or as a nattily attired businessman.

By nature he was as cruel and vicious as he was bold and resourceful. Never would he hesitate to kill if it was necessary for a getaway. The police said that he was incorrigible; that he had "crime in his blood." Yet, ironically, he was fond of children and was known to protect dumb animals from cruelty.

Typical of his operations was the robbery of a large Paris store near the Cathédral de Notre-Dame. It was in early February of 1947 when his career had reached its height. Breaking into the place long after closing hours, Buisson felled the night watchman, Ernest Belicaud, and killed him with a single shot when he screamed for help. Then he broke open the safe and fled with two million francs.

Less than a month later Buisson and his little gang in broad daylight waylaid a bank wagon at Fontenay-sous-Bois at the gates of Paris, beat the driver and his bodyguard, and escaped with a million francs.

While a frantic search was under way, the bandits appeared again, operating this time in a fast automobile. Two bank wagons were stopped in quick succession at Garenne-Colombes, also close to Paris, and their drivers beaten into insensibility. The loot, as before, totaled in excess of one million francs.

Only two weeks had passed when Buisson appeared again, this time at Troyes, with six confederates. Six bank employees were carrying two million francs through a busy street when the gang, armed and masked, pounced on them and escaped with their plunder. The robbery had taken less than a minute.

One of the victims fired at the fleeing bandits but missed. Buisson turned, returned the fire, and a man fell seriously wounded.

The area was soon surrounded. Roadblocks were set up but no trace of the robbers or their car could be found. Long afterward Chenevier learned the secrets of Buisson's strategy in such daring crimes. In the Troyes robbery Buisson, who knew the value of brothel keepers as accomplices, was informed of the habits of the bank messengers by the keeper of a house of ill fame located close to the bank. He then studied their route and carefully perfected a timetable for their movements up to the actual moment of the robbery. Anticipating that the highways would be guarded against escape, he directed one of his women accomplices to rent an apartment near the holdup scene where the bandits could hide until roadblocks had been removed. Obviously, the same practice was used in the other bank robberies.

Similar crimes continued at frequent intervals but as victims described the holdup men it again became apparent, as it had before, that Buisson rarely operated with the same men.

Through informers, Chenevier learned the answer—Buisson was ruthlessly killing his accomplices whenever he suspected disloyalty. More than ten had been shot down and buried in the forests.

One such victim of Buisson's cruel, premeditated executions was René Polledri, a Corsican who once had been a close and trusted member of the gang. He had been picked for death because of a few indiscreet words which caused Buisson to suspect that his friend could not be trusted. Not until months later did Chenevier learn the details of Polledri's fate.

After Buisson had fully decided that the man must die, he spent days planning an execution safe from police detection. He chose the scene—the Passage Landrieu—a dark, narrow Paris alley, seldom frequented. But Buisson, true to type, sardonically planned to wine and dine his victim before the hour of execution.

First he directed two of his most trusted men, Franck and Joyet, to be in the alley at precisely eleven o'clock the next night and to wait for him. He invited Polledri to be his guest at dinner in a restaurant near the alley. To make the last meal a gay party, he asked one of their mutual friends, a Corsican named Pierre Rosini, to join them. As a host, Buisson outdid himself, as was his custom on such occasions. For the condemned man and the other guest he ordered only the best in food and wine. It was a frivolous evening as the three recounted past experiences.

Suddenly Buisson looked at his watch. It was nearly 11:30. Rising to his feet, he proposed that they have their last drink and called on the waiter for more wine.

The host clicked glasses with Polledri, offering a toast "to your long life." A few minutes later they walked out of the eating place together.

"Let's take a little walk to get the stiffness out of our legs," Buisson suggested and the two guests unsuspectingly followed their host into the nearby alley. Suddenly they heard the sound of an automobile, unusual in the narrow street. At that moment, without a word, Buisson drew a revolver and sent three bullets into the man whose long life he had just toasted. Polledri fell dead as their companion, Rosini, ran for cover.

The machine pulled out with Boussin starting for the door but, with a sudden change of mind, he quickly turned and stepped beside the body. Poking his Colt into his victim's mouth, he fired again. "Now your tongue will squeal no more," he muttered, as he hurried to the car and vanished.

Polledri's body, slumped in the gutter, was found the following day. He was the only victim whose remains Buisson had not buried in the forest of Senart near Paris. Whether the others had died under similarly grim circumstances no one ever knew.

In August 1947, Chenevier learned through his well-trained informers that Buisson was hiding in the Paris outskirts. He led a posse to the place, surrounded it, and took the bandit leader without bloodshed. Buisson's wild career of crime appeared to have ended but he had other plans.

He was soon convicted and sentenced to life imprisonment at hard labor. However, his mind had been working fast. Realizing that it would be easier to escape from an asylum than a prison, he feigned insanity; he did it so well that highly respected alienists agreed that he should be moved to an insane asylum at Villejuif on the outskirts of Paris. It was now for his devoted brother, Jean Baptiste, to redeem their pledge of mutual assistance and through accomplices a plot was born.

Late in the night of September 3, Jean Baptiste drove a stolen automobile to a designated spot just outside of the high walls of the hospital. Jean threw a rope ladder over the wall and Emile escaped undetected.

The wave of desperate holdups was resumed to the consternation of Chenevier and the entire Sureté. Every resource of the French police was taxed in a frantic effort to apprehend the fugitive but they were outwitted at every turn.

For nearly three years—thirty-three months to be exact—the "most wanted man" in France defied capture. Boldly he slipped out of police nets time and again when Chenevier believed arrest to be a certainty. Daring robberies continued unabated.

Through informers Chenevier had learned that the

bandit's hiding place was within Paris limits but its exact location remained a mystery. Months of futile effort passed slowly to the chagrin of the authorities.

Not until March 1950 did Chenevier learn from his best and most trusted informer, a former convict, the exact whereabouts of the bandit he had hunted for thirty months and his shrewd mind began to ponder the safest and most effective course of action. Puzzling questions now confronted him. Should he lead a posse at once to the fugitive's hiding place and try to take him? Should he risk a gun battle and possible failure, perhaps Buisson's escape and the inevitable revenge murder of the informer? Would it be wiser to play a waiting game as he had done many times before, carefully planning to trap his quarry by surprise at a time and place when Buisson would be least expecting capture?

These and like problems Chenevier weighed thoughtfully, reckoning that Buisson, now more desperate than ever and trigger happy, was almost always on his guard, ready to shoot his way out of any trap and take the life of his betrayer. And in this case, the detective reasoned, Buisson would know that only one man, the informer, could have been the traitor.

In the end Chenevier decided against immediate action; he would play a cat and mouse game with the man he wanted. His conclusions were guided by several factors— his obligation to protect his faithful informer should capture fail, the danger of a heavy loss of life if immediate capture was attempted, and the hazard that should Buisson escape under gun fire he might not be located again for months or even years.

The game that Chenevier therefore chose to play lasted for more than two months until the detective, eight days before the capture, selected its exact place, hour and minute.

Chenevier still recalls his strategy, though many years have passed. "As soon as I knew where he was and had decided on my course, I planned deliberately to make him overconfident. Looking ahead with my plans in mind I foresaw the tenth of June at 1:45 in the afternoon as the time to spring my trap but I was mistaken by two minutes. It was 1:47 when he had the handcuffs on his wrists.

"I knew that Buisson was so intelligent, so clever, and so tricky that the slightest detail would let him know that he was being watched. Under my plan he was at my mercy for over two and a half months and every move I made was directed toward having him at the designated spot for his arrest at the hour that I had fixed. To achieve my purpose I used a method as old as the world—the Trojan Horse. I first sent for my cleverest 'stool-pigeon,' the one who had told me where in Paris Buisson was hiding, and I directed him to go to a cafe which he had told me Buisson sometimes frequented.

"The two—Buisson and my informer—had known each other in prison and Buisson trusted him implicitly. But under my orders the informer was not to contact him first; it was necessary under my plan that the gangster should get himself into my net; then he would not become suspicious.

"Such an operation is very delicate," Chenevier continues, "but I have always said a gangster is only human and left entirely alone, he is easier to capture. I knew that I was assuming a great risk. That is why I refused to share it even with my closest associates. It was a poker game between Buisson and myself. He was very clever but I was confident that I could maneuver him into one false move and then I would be the victor."

Long familiar with the ways of gangsters, Chenevier chose to gamble on his confidence that Buisson would remain true to type. "The day will come," the detective reasoned, "when Buisson will run out of money. That's when he'll follow all others of his kind; he'll plan a holdup;

he'll contact my informer who he knew in prison and offer him a share of the loot in return for a car and a gun."

He had reckoned well. Before too long Buisson approached the "stool-pigeon" in the cafe and made his proposition, just as Chenevier had predicted. In his own way, the informer succeeded in getting word to the detective.

"I let three days go by," Chenevier relates, "for quicker action would have aroused suspicions. Then I went to a garage and rented a small car—the type that Buisson preferred for holdups—and I saw that it got into the hands of my informer. I also sent him a loaded Colt. Then, through secret channels of my own, I arranged that Buisson be taken by my 'stoolie' to an inn in Paris where he could rest quietly before the robbery that had been planned."

At frequent intervals, word reached the detective that all was going well; the gangster was enjoying fine food and a rest.

One day, during this tense waiting period, Chenevier confided his plot to his aide and friend, Commissionaire Gilard, who could not refrain from voicing his disapproval and his fears.

"Do you realize the risk you're taking—playing such a game entirely by yourself?" Gilard exclaimed.

Chenevier assured him that he was not worried but Gilard was far from convinced. "Suppose your plans miscarry," he argued. "Suppose you don't take him and he's caught in a holdup with the car and the gun that you provided. That could not only end your career; it could make you liable for criminal action as an accomplice in a robbery. Your nerve well might cause the end of your career."

The detective grinned at his companion. "My dear fellow," he replied, "that is what the game of poker is. I can't catch Buisson without betting my entire pile. And, incidentally, you still don't know the whole story. I'm the one who paid for Buisson and the ex-convict at the inn."

The conversation ended with Chenevier's request that

Gilard send two picked inspectors to his office. When they met hours later, they were startled by Chenevier's blunt words.

"I simply want to announce to you," he said, "that at 1:45 on the afternoon of June 10 we are going to arrest Emile Buisson." Detailed instructions followed and when the two officers departed they knew just where they were to be stationed at the inn and what they were expected to do.

Early in the morning of the designated day, Chenevier drove alone over the Deauville route to a point close to the inn. He parked his car a distance away and walked through a forest until he reached a clump of shrubbery a few yards from the building. There Inspector Hours awaited him. The moment for final action was near.

Minutes later a flashy sports car of expensive make pulled up. It was a machine that Chenevier had carefully selected, for he knew of Buisson's peculiar interest in fine automobiles. Out of it stepped two inspectors in plain-clothes and a well-dressed woman, the wife of one of them.

Buisson, lunching at his favorite table overlooking the broad verandas, saw the costly machine and stood up to admire it.

The three newcomers selected a table close to Buisson and gave their orders. Then, at a moment that had been set well in advance, one of the inspectors turned to the waiter with a request, spoken loudly so that Buisson would over-hear. "Can you get me the reception clerk at the Hôtel Normandy at Deauville?" he asked. "I want to talk to him about reservations." The waiter stepped to a nearby tele-phone and Buisson, who had strained his ears to catch the conversation, leisurely resumed his meal.

The waiter soon beckoned to the inspector, Borniche, who left his seat, walked briskly by Buisson without a glance, and picked up the receiver. "Reception desk?" he inquired, again in a voice loud enough for Buisson's ears.

"This is Dr. André of Paris. I'd like to confirm the reservation for myself and wife. We'll arrive this evening for a week's stay."

"One moment, please," the clerk replied. "Let me check my book"—but "Dr. André" went on talking as had been planned. "Very good, very," he exclaimed as if he had been assured of accommodations. "What will be your rates for a room with twin beds and a bath?"

He was still speaking—for Buisson's benefit alone—when the clerk informed him that there were no reservations. "This, sir, is quite satisfactory," Borniche went on, ignoring what the hotel clerk had told him. "We are bringing some friends with us, Mr. and Mrs. Forestier. Could you reserve a room for them?"

The clerk, now more confused than ever, continued with apologies; there were no rooms for either "Dr. André" or his friends.

But the "Doctor" continued speaking, solely for the benefit of his nearby listener, Buisson. "That will be fine," he told the bewildered hotel man. "A room with twin beds will be fine and we'd like it to adjoin ours if possible."

As he hung up, the pseudo Mr. Forestier appeared—in reality Inspector Gilard. "Were you able to get a room for us?" he asked the "Doctor" in loud voice.

There was no response for at that precise moment the two officers seized the unsuspecting Buisson and told him that he was under arrest. Mrs. Borniche quickly put a whistle to her lips, the signal that Chenevier had been anxiously awaiting. In a flash he came bounding into the room—in time to hear the handcuffs click on the prisoner's wrists.

Buisson, his face white with rage, glared at the detective. "You again, Chenevier," he snarled.

"Yes, it's me," the other answered, looking at his watch. "It is now 1:47. I'm sorry to say that it's two minutes later than I had planned for this little meeting."

There followed a bizarre sequel, one that would not be found in fiction.

Both Chenevier and Inspector Hours had passed their luncheon time and excitement had added to their hunger. They took their places at the table beside the manacled Buisson and leisurely ordered their midday meal.

"Sit down with us, Mimile," Chenevier told his prisoner. "You have time for a cup of coffee and a brandy if you wish."

Buisson shook his head, staring angrily at the officers as they ate with relish. He spoke only once when Chenevier was served an order of fresh strawberries.

"Do you know where they came from?" Buisson inquired. "I picked them myself in the garden just this morning."

"Is that so," said the detective. "Anyway, they're excellent."

"If I had known you were going to eat them," said Buisson with a wry smile, "I'd have sprinkled them with rat poison."

Chenevier laughed; then in serious mood he asked his prisoner what had put him off his guard. "I think it was the car," he answered. "No one ever saw detectives riding in a machine like that; besides, your men were not known to me, so I wasn't suspicious for a second during that telephone talk."

His captor rose from his chair, put down his napkin and turned to the handcuffed man. "Let's get going, Mimile," he said quietly. "It's time now to think of more serious things."

With a sense of pride and triumph, Chenevier led the man to the waiting car. "I had won the last game with the 'great uncatchable,'" he still relates, as if only days had passed instead of years. "Bold and cynical, he was to be feared because he was always ready to go to any extreme. The police said that he never could be taken alive; that he would defend himself to the death. Perhaps that is why I wanted to bring him into the headquarters of the Sureté with handcuffs on his wrists."

On the ride to jail, Buisson reflected briefly on his ruined life. "What I have done," he told his captor, "there are only two who know—the good Lord and myself. Had my daughter lived I'm sure I would have straightened up." He had no more to say.

The law moved swiftly as if to compensate for the long years spent in bringing Emile Buisson to justice. This time he was sentenced to death.

At dawn on February 28, 1956, he walked to the guillotine in the courtyard of Santé Prison in Paris.

Chapter 11

Ohio's Ace Investigator
Ora E. Slater

On the morning of July 16, 1926, people across the country picked up their newspapers and read the first meagre report of a shocking midnight murder. In Canton, Ohio, the crusading editor of a daily newspaper had been shot from ambush in front of his own garage. It was the price that Don T. Mellett, a courageous thirty-six-year-old reformer, had paid for defying the underworld's repeated threats of death.

As the day wore on, details of the crime gradually unfolded. Mellett, with his wife and two friends, Mr. and Mrs. Walter Vail, had dined in the outskirts of Canton. They returned to his home shortly after midnight and while the women turned to preparing a snack, the editor walked outside to his car parked at the curb close by.

He drove into his garage in the rear of the house, closed one of the doors and was about to shut the other when two shots rang out and Mellett, with a gasp, slumped to the ground.

Four more shots followed in quick succession but missed their mark. Hearing the blasts, those in the house dashed through the front door to the garage and carried the unconscious man into his living room. A doctor was summoned but Mellett was already dead. He had been shot twice in the head with steel-jacket bullets.

In less than an hour the house was swarming with police

and newsmen. Search for footprints or other clues was unavailing and detectives, trying to reconstruct the crime, reasoned that the second volley had been fired to prevent Vail and the women from leaving the house by the rear door and perhaps sighting the killer in his flight.

Neighbors, who had hurried outdoors on hearing gunfire, told police that for several days they had seen a strange car lurking near the Mellett home. It bore a Pennsylvania license and was occupied by three men.

Tearfully, Mrs. Mellett reported that because of threatening letters, her husband had engaged a retired policeman to watch their home but the guard had been dismissed the night before the murder.

No one doubted that Mellett, editor and publisher of the *Canton Daily News*, owned by James M. Cox, the former Governor of Ohio, had been shot in revenge for his fearless, persistent attacks on underworld corruption and his bold charges of police collusion.

Three days prior to his death Mellett, answering a late night telephone call to his home, had listened to the words of a mysterious voice: "I'm going to get you, Mellett."

"No, you won't," he countered. "I'll get you first."

Months earlier Mellett had published a stinging editorial under his own name exposing two underworld characters and seven police officers for their involvement in bootleg activities. "They must be made to know that the game is about to end," he wrote.

In another article he had attacked the Civil Service Commission for its failure to rid the Police Department of crooked officers. The campaign continued with increasing vigor.

While these facts clearly established the murder motive, few in Canton believed that the police, bitterly resentful of Mellett's accusations, would bring the killer to justice. Before night of the first day of the tragedy spokesmen for the Scripps-Howard Newspapers in Ohio offered a $5000

reward for capture of the killer. An additional offer of
$25,000 was posted by a group of prominent citizens and
civic organizations.

The newspaper chain did still more. Thoroughly distrustful of the police, it contacted the Cal Crim Detective
Bureau in Cincinnati, requesting that its crack investigator,
Ora E. Slater, be sent to Canton to conduct a thorough
and independent investigation.

Slater, the publishers knew, was recognized as one of
the ablest, shrewdest detectives in the country, a human
dynamo whose lack of formal education was more than
balanced by his lightning brain, keen insight and amazing
memory. He was credited with an uncanny way of "looking
through people," quickly judging their character; and of
knowing just how to bore into puzzling cases to ferret out
the truth. On occasion, in vital interrogations, he bluffed
but he knew just when and how to do it. Rarely did
such strategy fail.

He could recall minor details of events long passed.
Some said that he could "smell a crook" from a distance.
His memory for faces was surprising. Once he hailed by
name a passerby on a Cincinnati street—a man he had
met for only a few minutes five years before in a prison
yard.

He understood human values and knew just when to be
tough or to appear soft and sympathetic—an ability that
he once demonstrated when he was on the staff of the
Indiana Reformatory. A supposedly "hardened" prisoner
had defied all efforts to obtain a confession to a series of
robberies. Slater begged for a chance to try.

First smoking with the man, Slater quickly found that
behind a gruff exterior lay a sensitive, sentimental vein.
He talked to the prisoner of various things—life, death and
home. The conversation was resumed the following day and
Slater turned it to family ties. Suddenly a band outside
struck up the strains of "Home, Sweet Home." The prisoner

broke into sobs and confessed. Slater then walked outside and paid the bandmaster he had hired for ten minutes. "Sugar captures more crooks than vinegar," Slater commented.

He afterward became a detective for the Big Four Railroad, a post in which he showed rare acumen and fearlessness by capturing a gang of rebellious laborers single-handed after their attempt to wreck a train.

He was later elected sheriff and when his term ended he joined the staff of Cal Crim, a popular Cincinnati detective, who had opened a private agency following his retirement. In this capacity, only months before the Mellett murder, Slater had won fame by quickly solving the mysterious bathtub murder of a housewife in the city of Troy. It was this achievement, above all else, that prompted his summons to Canton.

Responding to the call on the Mellett case, Slater arrived in Canton while a mournful crowd, gathered at the editor's funeral, heard his employer, former Governor Cox, deliver a touching eulogy. "I never knew finer moral courage than his," Cox said. "He was driving the messengers of evil to their lair and these persons decided that he must die."

When the services had ended and Mellett had been lowered in his grave, Slater went directly to the office of the Stark County Prosecutor, C. B. McClintock. He introduced himself and took a chair while the lawyer gazed curiously in the ruddy face of a man in his early fifties, with graying hair and eyes that seemed to cover the room in a single sweep. Slater was dressed conservatively and McClintock told himself that his visitor looked more like a country undertaker than a detective.

"I've been engaged by the Scripps-Howard Newspapers," Slater announced.

"That may be," remarked the prosecutor, smiling, "but you're going to work for me."

"Work for you?" Slater asked incredulously.

"That's it," the other rejoined. "I know what you did in that bathtub case and I've phoned the newspaper people. They've agreed to release you to this office. You'll be my man in charge of the case. They'll foot the bill."

Their talk continued and Slater, who always chose to get the initial, basic facts of a case directly from the most logical source, finally announced that he would begin by interviewing the widow. McClintock summoned Earl Hexamer, the county safety director, and the three drove away.

Slater listened attentively as Mrs. Florence Mellett tearfully related details of the shooting, explaining that her husband had lived in expectation of death. "Only a few days ago," she said, "Don told me: 'If anything happens to me I want you to bear up. I am marked for death but I am a fatalist. What's coming is coming.'"

The detective asked her a few specific questions and then departed, stating that for a time he would like to wander about alone "to get the feel of the situation." It was a practice he often followed when first coming to grips with a puzzling case. He said it gave him a chance to think and sometimes to speak casually with townspeople in no way involved in the matter.

That night in his room in the McKinley Hotel he dropped into an easy chair, took off his shoes and lit a cigarette, eager to review in his mind the day's events. He already had learned many things. For one, Mellett's murder had been the seventeenth in that county in recent years; fourteen of them in Canton.

People to whom he spoke were severely critical of the police, yet they seemed afraid to discuss more than generalities and it was obvious that many were withholding information. He learned further that the murdered editor was ready to prove that Canton police were under orders to protect bawdy houses and gambling places in the city's tenderloin, popularly called the Jungle. And he was told that the fatal bullets were of the type used by the police.

What surprised him perhaps still more was the attitude of substantial citizens. The tragedy, far from uniting them in helping to solve the murder, had split the community into rival groups. Meetings, called hurriedly by civic bodies, had broken up into bitter factions. H. H. Timken, a millionaire manufacturer and a man of influence, had failed in a dramatic plea for unity.

Slater started out again early the next morning and as he slowly pieced together scraps of information, he became aware of a conspiracy between Canton bootleggers and certain police officers. Profits were enormous. Equally lucrative, he had learned, were the earnings of brothels, dives and gambling places operating with protection in the Jungle.

He called on Mellett's brother, Lloyd, the city editor of the *Daily News,* and before he left he had the name of his first suspect. "You should know," Lloyd told him, "that a week ago a notorious figure in the underworld—Louis Mazer—called on Don in his office while I was sitting there. He was angry about a story Don had printed and demanded a retraction. Don simply told him off and as Mazer walked off I heard him say: 'I know how to take care of guys like you.'"

Slater wrote the name in his notebook, determined to learn everything about the man without giving him any cause to suspect that he was under investigation. Before long, however, the detective had added a second name, that of Patrick E. McDermott, also a familiar figure in the Jungle. He bought a newspaper and was surprised to read a statement by the reputed "king" of the tenderloin, "Jumbo" Crowley, who vigorously denied any part in the murder. Others of his ilk were also publicly proclaiming innocence and Slater began to wonder the significance of their eagerness for vindication.

Then he sent to Cincinnati for two operatives, intending to have them trail his two suspects as a routine course. His own effort would be in a different direction, for Slater always believed that clues should lead to suspects rather than the reverse.

At this point he decided that it was time to follow his usual practice of calling on the authorities after he had carefully surveyed the scene by himself.

He went to the office of the Chief of Police, Seranus Lengel, who a short time before had sued Mellett for $50,000 damages over an editorial. Lengel greeted his visitor warmly and spoke discouragingly of the case. "We're really up against a stone wall," he said. "We've questioned over fifty suspects and no soap. This was an out of town job. You can't pin anything on the underworld."

They were still conversing when Lengel suddenly jumped to his feet. "I didn't kill him," he exclaimed excitedly. "I couldn't shoot a dog." Then, noting the surprised look on the other's face, he added: "I know there are some who are talking, but I swear I didn't do it. Mellett did everything to ruin me but I licked him every time. My conscience is clear."

Concealing his amazement over such a plea of innocence, this time from the Chief himself, Slater casually inquired whether there were any clues. Before the Chief could answer his door opened and a tall, heavily-built man walked in. He was introduced as Floyd Streitenberger, chief of the detective force, who Slater had been told was "one strictly honest cop."

"Streity," as the Chief called him, was told of Slater's mission. Then, reaching into his wallet, he took out a Western Union wire and handed it to the man from Cincinnati, explaining that he had found it in Mellett's coat pocket. With a Pittsburgh dateline, it said tersely: LAST WARNING TO LAY OFF. YOU KNOW WHO.

"Strange they accepted such a message," Slater remarked. "I'd really like to know what the sender looked like."

"No problem," Streitenberger snapped, with something of a smirk. He already had the answer: "He was a youngish man, dark complexioned; simply told the Western Union clerk that he was playing a joke on a friend." Then the Chief, obviously eager to establish his own efficiency, showed Slater the original of the message which had come from Pittsburg. His visitor looked at it and smiled. "Block letters," he commented. "The old trick to conceal handwriting. If you don't mind I'll take it with me for a day or two."

Starting out again, Slater moved slowly over downtown streets, eager to be alone once more to ponder over what had just occurred and to consider what he should do next. Streitenberger's manner, especially his self-assurance, puzzled him and he wondered whether he had been misinformed about the officer's integrity.

Slater had not gone far when he suddenly observed that two men were trailing him. Hours later they followed him into his hotel and he was informed that they were henchmen for underworld figures. He stepped up to the pair and told them angrily: "Listen, you birds, you've tailed me long enough. I'm going across town and if you follow me it will be just too bad."

With that he turned on his heels and walked away. The others did not follow but on his return to the hotel he found a note that read: "If you know what's good for you you'll get out of town or you'll get what Mellett got."

The warning, like the message left in the Pittsburgh telegraph office, was in block letters done firmly with a soft black pencil, and Slater reasoned that both had been done by the same person who had sent the telegram from Pennsylvania presumably to make it appear that the plot had been hatched in another state.

By now he believed that the murderer was a hired gunman, probably from out of town. Putting himself in the killer's role, he reckoned that the man would have studied Mellett's habits to determine the best time and place to strike. He already had a fair description of a loiterer around the office of the *Daily News*. It matched the image of a stranger seen close to the Mellett home, sometimes on foot, at other times in the parked machine with two companions.

Assuming that this person was the imported gunman, Slater determined to learn where he had stayed. He sent again to Cincinnati for more operatives and while they visited lodging houses and cheap hotels, the detective went to Pittsburgh for a personal talk with the Western Union clerk, hoping for a more accurate description of the man who had sent the wire.

The trip was fruitful, for the clerk, taxing his memory, recalled details that the police detective had not mentioned. He now remembered the stranger's peculiar haircut, the shape of his nose, and a scar on his face. At once Slater's quick wit and resourcefulness went into action. Availing himself of the clerk's willingness to cooperate, he turned to the young man with a simple proposal. "You can help me still further," he said. "If I brought someone over here to draw a picture of this fellow from your description would you work with him?" The clerk readily agreed.

That evening Slater returned with a commercial artist who drew a composite portrait of the stranger from the description given him. The clerk looked at it with surprise. "Say, that's him all right," he exclaimed. "Couldn't be a better likeness if this guy had posed for it."

Slater returned to Canton and showed the drawing to Streitenberger with whom he now had established friendly accord but the result was disappointing. "Streity" said the portrait resembled someone he believed he might have seen in the tenderloin but he did not know the name nor did he show much interest.

More encouraging word came from Slater's operatives who had been checking rooming houses for a clue to an out of town gunman. They had located a place where a man registered as Charles Thompson had stayed until his hurried departure the morning after the murder. He had said that he was from Pittsburgh.

Reckoning that this lead supported his theory of an imported gunman, Slater went to the place to interview the landlady and his visit started a chain of rapid events. From the woman he learned that Thompson had made a number of long distance telephone calls. Contacting the telephone company, he was told that all of them had been to a restaurant in Cleveland.

Slater drove there and found that the recipient of Thompson's calls was a waitress named Peggy Cavanaugh, who knew little of the man excepting that she had served him some weeks before and had accepted his invitation for an auto ride to Akron. This seemed of little interest until the girl remarked casually that, in Akron, Thompson had stopped by a pharmacy to make a phone call.

When she recalled the date of her jaunt, the detective persuaded her to drive with him to Akron and point out the drug store. Again he checked with the telephone company. The call had been made to a well-known bawdy house in the Canton Jungle.

Because experience told him that the remotest hunch sometimes brings surprises, Slater stationed one of his men near the house with the drawing made by the artist. There was a remote chance, he thought, that the man who had sent the wire from Pittsburgh might appear.

Two days passed before a man closely resembling the portrait walked into the house, remained a time, and left in a taxi. The operative, in another cab, followed to the outskirts of Massillon, a town near Canton, but the first machine was suddenly lost in traffic.

Never one to give up, Slater followed another hunch and showed his composite picture to the police chief in Massillon. "Know anybody who looks like this?" he inquired.

The Chief's face brightened. "Of course I do," he said. "That's young Rudner—Ben Rudner. His father's a millionaire and he's had plenty of trouble with that kid. He was sent up to Leavenworth for rum running, came out and his old man set him up here in a hardware store. They say he's going straight."

Slater, however, was not so certain in spite of Detective Streitenberger's insistence that Rudner could not be the man who had sent the threatening wire from Pittsburgh. "I know he's on the level now," said "Streity." "You can scratch him off your list." Nevertheless Slater gave orders to have Rudner trailed.

The detective's keen deduction powers went to work again. "If Rudner did time in Leavenworth," he reasoned, "someone up there should know who were his pals in the bootleg game." So Slater went to the penitentiary. Officials there remembered Rudner well and recalled that his closest friend had been Pat McDermott who came from Chicago and was a gunman.

Obtaining McDermott's prison pictures, Slater returned to Canton and showed them to the Mellett neighbors. They were positive that McDermott was the stranger they had seen loitering about the murdered editor's home.

By now Slater was convinced that both Rudner and McDermott were involved but the pattern of the plot was lacking and he was certain that it included others. Before long he became more suspicious of Louis Mazer, the pool-room owner who had threatened Mellett in his office. Slater's operative, watching Rudner's store, had seen Mazer frequenting the place.

To satisfy his curiosity, Slater called on Detective Streitenberger at his home late one night to inquire about Mazer. "Oh, he's okay," the officer said, rushing to the man's defense. "Sure, he's got a record but he's learned his lesson. Don't waste your time on him."

The two sat down to discuss other aspects of the case and through Slater's mind ran a recollection of "Streity's" earlier effort to vindicate Rudner. It was more than the detective could understand. As he rose to go, the officer's police dog limped into the living room and "Streity" remarked that his pet had been sick for days. Slater thought nothing of the incident until the following afternoon.

He had driven to Rudner's store to look around. A cab pulled up and its driver carried a sick dog into the place. It was Streitenberger's pet. Neighbors told Slater that Rudner was something of a veterinarian but an association between a police detective and a former convict was puzzling.

When he saw "Streity" again he inquired about the dog. "He's worse," the officer said. "I took him to a hospital two days ago." There was no mention of Rudner's name and Slater came to further doubt the honesty of the "honest cop."

Now, he believed, the time had come for drastic action. Federal officials had joined the state authorities in the investigation, demanding a cleanup of vice and Slater had been assured of all necessary cooperation. He decided that the situation called for wire-tapping; Streitenberger, Rudner and Mazer were singled out for such attention.

His patience was rewarded a few nights later when "Streity" received a call from Pittsburgh. In an angry voice the caller introduced himself as "Mac" and said he was tired of waiting for his money. The officer promised payment; warned him not to call again, and the conversation ended. The policeman immediately relayed the message to Mazer who said that the money would be sent to "Mac" in a few days. "I can't stall him much longer," the officer said. "Just remember, I hired him for the job."

Slater by now was thoroughly satisfied that McDermott, Rudner and Mazer were heavily involved in the murder and he decided to turn the case over to the prosecutor. Before he could contact that official, however, he received an unexpected visit from a stranger, Steve Koschalk, who said he wanted to divulge what he knew and relieve his mind. His disclosures soon added new support to Slater's conclusions.

Koschalk came directly to the point. "I want to tell you about Pat McDermott," he began. "I met him on a street-car in Cleveland and we went to Massillon together. The next day he asked me if I would beat up a man for $500 and I said I would. Later we met Ben Rudner who talked about Mellett and he told me there was money in it for anyone who'd give him a good beating. That night Mazer joined us and we drove by the Mellett house several times, but I finally told them I didn't want anything to do with their business. They called me a 'yellow rat,' so I left them and I haven't seen them since."

Slater was still turning Koschalk's story over in his mind when a couple, William and Eva Betzler, called on him with further information. Betzler had met McDermott, an old Army friend, in the latter's rooming house. There McDermott displayed a revolver and said he was going to be well paid for "a job." Betzler also cleared an important point that had been worrying the detective. McDermott had stayed at the same place where Slater's men had located Thompson and he was registered under the latter name. Only hours after the murder he had vanished.

After these disclosures Slater called on the prosecutor, McClintock, reviewing all that he had learned and it was decided that the entire case with all of its amazing ramifications should be presented to a specially impaneled grand jury. More than fifty witnesses, located and previously interrogated by Slater, were summoned. Mazer and Rudner were among them. Sessions consumed several days and nights and though the jurors were pledged to secrecy it became known that some of the witnesses had made startling admissions, disclosing intimate details of the murder plot.

The grand jury's final action fell like a lightning bolt on Canton and on all of Ohio for the jurors had agreed that the men participating in the plot as conspirators were as guilty as those who had fired the lethal bullets. Indictments charging first degree murder were returned against the following:

Chief of Police Seranus Lengel.

Detective Floyd Streitenberger, Chief of the Detective Force.

Patrick McDermott, the triggerman.

Ben Rudner and Louis Mazer.

The accused were promptly arrested excepting McDermott who had disappeared. Rudner and Mazer asserted that they could establish alibis. Streitenberger soon confessed that he had been one of the instigators of the plot in which, he said, Chief Lengel had played an important role.

Lengel previously had been suspended by Mayor S. M. Swarts, who accused him of bungling and of permitting suspects to mingle with the police during the investigation.

McDermott became the object of a nationwide search and trial of the others was deferred pending his arrest.

Three months later Slater, learning that the fugitive was hiding in Cleveland, contacted the accused man's brothers and urged them to negotiate for his surrender. They finally succeeded but McDermott stubbornly insisted that he was innocent. Many believed that fear of underworld retaliation had induced him to keep silent. His was the first of a series of sensational trials packed with drama. Testifying in his own behalf before Judge F. M. Diehl, he contended that he was the victim of a frameup, a plea that failed to impress the jury which found him guilty of first degree murder with a recommendation for mercy. It was Christmas Eve.

Minutes later McDermott heard himself sentenced to life imprisonment in Ohio State Penitentiary. Turning to his lawyers he made a single comment:

"A hell of a Christmas present to give a guy."

Rudner, next brought to trial, was convicted of second

degree murder and likewise was sentenced to spend the balance of his life with McDermott in state's prison.

After these two convictions, Mazer suddenly had a change of heart and made a full confession, later turning state's evidence as a star witness against Detective Streitenberger.

"Honest Streity" was found guilty of murder and sent to prison for life. Mazer, as a reward for his testimony, escaped with a sentence of from five to twenty years.

Last of the conspirators to face a jury was Chief of Police Lengel, who soon after the murder had startled Slater with an unsolicited plea of innocence. Now, in a crowded courtroom he squirmed nervously in his chair as his one-time best friend in the department, Streitenberger, testified that Lengel was a party to the conspiracy that began with plans to beat the editor and ended with his slaying. The jury found the former Chief guilty of murder but its recommendation of mercy saved him from the electric chair.

Before being sentenced to life imprisonment, Lengel rose and asked permission to make a statement. With his eyes turned heavenward, he exclaimed:

"May God strike me dead if, as I stand here, I am guilty of this charge."

Six months later, however, the Ohio State Supreme Court granted Lengel a new trial and Streitenberger was brought from the penitentiary to appear again as the state's star witness. When he flatly refused to testify the court threatened contempt proceedings but the man already under a life sentence was not impressed. After the state had closed its case, the court ordered a directed verdict of acquittal and Lengel walked away a free man. He died in Cleveland, January 8, 1941, at the age of seventy-one.

Slater's brilliant career continued until his death in 1945 at the age of seventy. Success in many other cases added to his fame but his earlier achievement in solving the bath-tub murder should be told for it was this that led to his assignment to the Mellett mystery only five months later.

The victim was an attractive housewife, Mrs. Frances Nesbitt, whose battered body was found submerged in the bathtub of her home in Troy, Ohio, on the morning of February 20, 1926. There were ugly wounds on her head and body. Fragments of her wrist watch, scattered over the floors of three rooms, told their story of the woman's desperate struggle with her slayer. No weapon was found and her husband, Jacob, who said he had discovered her body, insisted that he could not account for motive since nothing in the apartment had been taken.

After two weeks of futile work by the police, Slater was summoned. He was told that several neighbors and even one or two friends suspected Nesbitt, since the couple was known to have quarreled frequently, but the husband claimed to have an airtight alibi, contending that he had found the body when he returned home from Dayton. However, he had been evasive when pressed for a corroborating witness.

Although Slater knew little more of the case, it intrigued him and he recognized it as one that would challenge not only his investigative methods but his way of probing the minds of men.

"I'll undertake the job," he said, "if Nesbitt will agree to cooperate with me in running down the murderer. If he is innocent, he should have no fear of working with me. In fact, he should be eager to do so."

Slater fully realized the difficulties he was facing, yet he was confident that his innate ability to judge character and human nature would help materially in determining Nesbitt's guilt or innocence, aside from an intensive investigation of the case itself.

Nesbitt, informed of Slater's proposal, said he was eager to work with a skilled detective. A meeting between the two was arranged but first Slater wanted to confer at length with detectives who had worked on the case. They told him that the husband's alibi could not be shaken. Supporting it was the fact that the hands of the woman's watch pointed to twelve. This and the condition of the body indicated that she had been murdered at noon of the previous day, a time when her husband claimed to have been at work.

Slater and Nesbitt met by appointment in the home of the wife's parents and the husband seemed to take a quick liking to the genial detective with a pleasant smile. During their initial conversation Slater was impressed by what appeared to be Nesbitt's sincere way of speaking and he noted that the man often looked him squarely in the eye. However, he realized that it was far too soon to draw conclusions; that he must see much more of the man when they could be alone before he could really judge him. It did not take him long to evolve a plan.

"Let me suggest something," he said to the husband. "I've just heard that a woman in Urbana had a time with a prowler who assaulted her and got away. Let's drive up there and talk to her. There just might be a connection with your case."

Nesbitt readily agreed, not suspecting Slater's real purpose, and they decided to leave early the following morning.

The trip was unproductive with the detective still unable to evaluate the man's real character. On the next day Slater learned of a letter received by Mrs. Nesbitt's parents from Warren, Ohio, 227 miles away. *"If you will send that Cincinnati detective here,"* the note read, *"I will tell him who killed Frances Nesbitt."*

While Slater discounted the message as the type often written at the height of murder mysteries, he was anxious to satisfy his curiosity, and, besides, another trip with Nesbitt would give him further opportunity to observe the man in close contact.

Slater deliberately arranged to leave Troy in the evening so that an overnight stop would be necessary. It was near midnight when they pulled up to a small hotel and Nesbitt's behavior suddenly became so strange that the detective's suspicions were aroused for the first time. "I think I'm being followed," the husband said, and it was apparent that he was highly agitated. He looked furtively about, then hurried into their room, slammed the door and bolted it. While Slater feigned a laugh, suggesting that his companion needed rest, he wondered whether Nesbitt's nerves were upset by a guilty conscience; whether he was feigning fear in an effort to conceal his real emotions. The two retired and as Slater glanced at the man in the bed beside him, he asked himself whether he might be sleeping with a murderer.

They arose early, breakfasted, and started for the home of the letter writer. Nesbitt appeared to have completely regained his composure. However, a change came abruptly while the two were conversing casually about the woman they were to visit. "I hope you won't mind," Slater was saying, "but this woman said she wanted to see me alone."

Suddenly Nesbitt became excited and this time it was clearly apparent that he was highly nervous. "I'd certainly like to hear what she has to say," he remarked, and the detective noted that the man's hands were twitching.

Slater quickly grasped the significance of this behavior. He proposed that his companion wait in a nearby service station until the woman had been met and asked if she objected to a third party's presence. Nesbitt reluctantly agreed and was soon beckoned to join the other two. The writer of the letter, it developed, was a friend of a fortune teller who lived upstairs and the three went to her apartment.

This woman, affecting a mystic air, put a match to a jar of incense and proceeded with weird gestures. For a time she peered silently into a crystal globe. "A woman killed Mrs. Nesbitt," she said slowly, pausing between the words.

"Why?" Slater pressed.

"She killed Mrs. Nesbitt because she was infatuated with her husband."

Nesbitt's eyes lit up and in an instant he looked like a different person; like a man from whose shoulders a weight suddenly had been lifted. Slater caught the change, realized its meaning, and his quick mind reacted to his opportunity. "No woman killed Mrs. Nesbitt," he asserted firmly, his sharp eyes fixed on the husband. "A man killed her—that I know."

Nesbitt's jaw dropped and it was obvious that he was trying hard to conceal his emotions. At once Slater, realizing the effectiveness of his daring bluff, followed with a question directed at the woman: "What was the color of the bloody comb found in her bathroom?"

The fortune teller shook her head and Nesbitt turned quickly away.

On the return trip he seldom spoke, appearing to be deeply absorbed in thought. Slater, however, had reached his own conclusions and decided to continue with his bluffing game as he had done successfully in similar situations. He realized the risk though he firmly believed that the end would justify the means. But first he must try to further weaken the other's nerves.

The highway turned and skirted a railroad track. A distance further Slater spied eleven wooden crosses, obviously marking the scene of a fatal accident. "Look at them," he remarked to his companion, pointing to the markers. "Poor souls, I wonder who they were; what they looked like."

"Yes," Nesbitt said without further comment.

"What do you imagine they were thinking of just before they died—just before they went into eternity?" Slater continued.

There was no response.

They rode on in silence and an hour later, passing a cemetery, the detective again talked of death and the mystery of life. Nesbitt listened silently and it was apparent now that he was fully aware of Slater's suspicions.

When they finally returned to Troy, the two men parted. Nesbitt went to the home of his wife's parents; Slater returned to his hotel and from there telephoned to two of Nesbitt's friends, C. C. Willard and H. L. Johnston.

"I want you to be at Nesbitt's home tomorrow afternoon at 1:30," he told each man. "I'll have Jake there and if I'm not mistaken we'll have a solution of the murder. But I ask just one thing of you—if he appeals to you for help, if he asks if you think he's innocent, I don't want a word of sympathy from you."

The three met in Nesbitt's apartment at the appointed time. Nesbitt eyed them nervously, wondering the reason for the gathering. The detective broke the silence.

"Nesbitt," he began bluntly, "you killed your wife. I've hunted all over for the other man and I know he just doesn't exist. You killed your wife and you know it."

"No, no," Nesbitt cried. "These friends here know I didn't do it, don't you?"

In answer they gave him an icy stare. No words were spoken and the frantic husband's renewed appeals likewise fell on deaf ears. Now Slater spoke again:

"Jake, you'd better tell the truth; you'd better tell it in the presence of your friends. You'll need friends when you go to trial."

Nesbitt wet his lips but made no comment. Then, as he listened tensely, Slater reviewed the husband's statements to the police. "You told them," he said sharply, "that on the morning of the murder you'd been demonstrating at a food show in Dayton. You expected to meet your wife there that morning but she didn't come. So you returned to Troy later in the day and went to her parents' home thinking she was there. And when your mother-in-law said she wasn't there, you entered the house to phone your wife at your own home. Is that correct?"

The husband nodded.

Now Slater was on his feet determined to bluff again. "You're lying," he shouted. "You weren't at that food show in the morning and you didn't do any of the things you say you did. You're simply telling a bunch of lies and you know it. Now then, tell us the truth."

There was no answer and Slater followed quickly with another question: "Do you remember combing your hair in the bathroom after kissing your wife goodby?"

"Yes."

The detective reached into his pocket and took out an envelope. "Here's that comb. Look at it. The chemists examined it and found stains of human blood. And how about that note you left her—'Don't forget to make a payment on the radio.' Why did you write that if you had kissed her goodby? Why didn't you just tell her? You're lying—you might as well admit it."

Nesbitt squirmed in silence. The detective went on, speaking slowly, his finger pointed at the accused man.

"Remember, some friends stayed all night with you and your wife two nights before the murder. You told the police you slept that night in your underwear because your pajamas were hanging in the bathroom and you couldn't get them. You said you were wearing your wife's pink kimono that you gave her for Christmas. But when you went into the guest room to raise a window, your friends noticed blue pajamas under the kimono. Where are those pajamas now?

"So you won't tell us," Slater pressed on. "You will before I'm finished with this case. There's enough evidence to convict you now and when the district attorney gets you on the stand, you'll wish you had these two friends to help you. I'm calling the police now—and then I'm forgetting that you ever lived."

There was silence for tense minutes. Slater rose, reaching for the telephone.

"No, don't call," Nesbitt screamed. "I—killed—her. I'll tell you why."

Nesbitt reached into his pocket for a handkerchief and wiped his forehead. "We'd been quarreling pretty badly just before it happened," he went on. "In fact, we weren't getting along at all. You see, both of us had been selling kitchen utensils. My wife was always complaining that I wasn't holding up my end and that I should look for a better job.

"That last night we were quarreling long after bedtime and she refused to let me in our bedroom. Next morning we were at it again, worse than ever. It went on for hours. Finally she made a mean remark about my family—said they were all an illiterate bunch. I slapped her; she slapped me back and then—well, everything seemed to turn black."

"The pajamas?" Slater demanded. "What became of them?"

"They had blood on them and I burned them in the furnace."

"And the comb?"

"I didn't realize there was blood on that."

Slater rose from his chair, walked to the telephone, and called the police.

Chapter 12

Crime Scientist

Edward Oscar Heinrich

Tiny pin pricks in the yellowed pages of a worn pulp magazine and the writing of the letter "t" in cryptic words penned invisibly in lemon juice once became the most pivotal and controversial factors in a series of damage suits totaling $55,000,000.

The issue arose long after World War I during a bitter years-long legal struggle between the United States Government and American industries on the one side and Germany on the other. It developed from one of the most devastating explosions in the nation's history—a series of terrific blasts that demolished more than 1000 tons of ammunition on Black Tom Island, a half-mile strip of land projecting from the New Jersey shore opposite the Statue of Liberty. The war supplies were awaiting shipment to the Allies; Uncle Sam had not yet entered the war.

Probably never before had an explosion of such magnitude rocked so wide an area and terrified so many people. Coming precisely at 2:08 o'clock of Sunday morning, July 30, 1916, it severely shook all of Manhattan, Brooklyn, and Jersey City, though it was felt as far as Philadelphia. In the New York and New Jersey areas, huge buildings trembled as if shaken by a giant hand; glass worth more than a million dollars was shattered.

On the streets pedestrians were thrown from their feet; in homes many were tossed forcefully from their beds.

Wreckage lay everywhere yet no one seemed to know just where the blasts had occurred or what had caused them. Some, in panic, gazed at the blood-red skies, convinced that the Kaiser's forces were invading. Hours passed before a frightened populace could be calmed.

Years later the disaster was to provide one of the most famous cases in the long and colorful career of a detective far across the continent, in Berkeley, California—Edward Oscar Heinrich. Time and again he was to traverse the country to offer expert judgment on the pin pricks in the magazine pages and the writing of the letter "t" until his opinions would be accepted as the final word, placing full blame for the explosions on German saboteurs and ending, once and for all, the prolonged litigation over financial responsibility for the holocaust, which took six lives and injured hundreds.

For Heinrich, recognized as the American pioneer in scientific crime detection, this was only one of many baffling cases that won him world-wide fame. Though his career began as a poorly-paid pharmacist's clerk, he had mastered many sciences, steadily developing his wide range of knowledge as his later work demanded. He finally became, in one, a biochemist, a geologist, a physicist, a handwriting expert, and an authority on inks and papers, to list only a few of his accomplishments. People called him the "Edison of Crime Detection," explaining that he could learn more from less than any other man. It was his contention that in every crime its perpetrator leaves his card behind; that it remains only for the detective to examine the scene thoroughly and to intelligently interpret what he has found.

Often in his long career as a criminologist, Heinrich had wrung secrets from a lone hair or a single bit of thread. Once he brought about the capture of three murderous train robbers—the d'Autremont brothers—through a few chips of fir that he found in the pocket of an abandoned pair of overalls. This case, like his work in the

Black Tom disaster, is recorded as another of his most notable achievements.

From early youth he had worked his way, from newsboy in his native city, Clintonville, Wisconsin, to professor of criminology at the University of California. In the interim, he had qualified himself to become city chemist of Tacoma, Washington, a position that led him into scientific crime detection. It was at a time when crime laboratories were not in general use and when peace officers knew little of the role that science plays in their work today.

As Heinrich developed his laboratory skills, solving important cases with test tubes and microscopes, law-enforcement officers from federal and local governments began coming to him with their problems. In time he became a national authority in his new field.

With such a background, Heinrich was selected from many others to play a major and expert role in drawing hidden secrets from meagre evidence in the Black Tom mystery—evidence that strangely did not come to light until years after the disaster. In the long interval much had taken place in and out of courts while American and German criminologists wrangled over evidence and theories.

The inquiry had started on Black Tom Island, the shipping terminal for the Lehigh Valley Railroad, whose tracks extended over a causeway to seven large brick warehouses and covered piers where vast quantities of war materials worth millions, were stored, pending their removal on lighters to Gravesend Bay. From there they were transferred to freighters bound for Allied depots overseas.

On the weekend of the holocaust, the Lehigh warehouses and docks were loaded with war supplies—dynamite, TNT, shrapnel, acids, and gasoline. The saboteurs had well-timed their ghastly plot.

The first blast had been followed by another seventeen minutes later and smaller explosions continued for hours. Warehouses blew up and freight cars burned like tinder.

Curious crowds, watching the flames from New York's Battery, were showered with flying bolts and other metal. On Ellis Island buildings were flattened and six hundred terrified immigrants were removed to safety.

Sabotage or accident at once became the vital question as hundreds of local and state police swarmed about the area when the debris began to cool but it was not long before all agreed that the explosions had resulted from a deliberate and well-organized plot of saboteurs. Suspicion soon fell on German agents, known to be active on the Atlantic seaboard and elsewhere in America, but at the start there was only theory and no evidence.

Before long the intensive investigation had assumed world-wide proportions with secret service agents of six nations hunting clues. Damage suits against Lehigh and other companies involved were filed, opening the way for litigation that continued for almost a quarter of a century, filling dozens of volumes with trial transcript.

Not until June 1939—a full twenty-three years after the explosions—was the case finally settled by the Mixed Claims Commission with a decision that reversed an earlier ruling and declared in favor of 153 American claimants. The Lehigh Railroad and many others had won at last—and Heinrich's expert findings had played a major role in bringing this about.

The story of the long investigation, with mysterious figures moving on and off the stage, is told in many musty volumes now stored in the Law Library of Columbia University. There was, for instance, a young Slovakian, Michael Kristoff, with a weird account of how he had accompanied a stranger for whom he carried a suitcase filled with pictures of bridges and factories. Explosions always followed their wanderings but Kristoff could not identify his employer and the trail was finally abandoned. Other suspects, equally mysterious, engaged detectives in months of inquiry that also came to nothing.

Six months of futile work had passed when, in January of the following year, the Kingsland Plant of thirty-eight buildings in the Jersey meadows blew up and again the blame fell on German agents when detectives learned that many of the Kaiser's spies were employed in the establishment.

Scarcely had the plant been rebuilt than a new attempt to blast it was thwarted and this time suspicion pointed to a man high in the German secret service who had held an important post at Kingsland. Eventually he and his associates were linked to the Black Tom explosions but all of them had disappeared.

Still more munitions plants went up in flames—a final total of ninety-nine—and as the inquiry progressed the pattern of the German sabotage network emerged more clearly than before.

On August 10, 1922, the Mixed Claims Commission for the United States and Germany was created to settle claims resulting from the war. At once Lehigh, Bethlehem Steel, insurance companies and many others pressed their claims, demanding that they be reimbursed for damages aggregating more than $55,000,000.

Hearings went on for years while the net appeared to tighten about new figures in and out of Germany. One discovery, perhaps more than any other, buoyed the hopes of claimants—an official cable in code from Berlin to the Embassy at Washington giving specific instructions for the campaign of destruction in America. There were other developments of this nature but the Commission finally decided, on October 16, 1930, that the American claims had not been proven and the decision went to Germany. The investigation, however, continued.

At length two men emerged as undoubtedly the most important witnesses for the Americans. One was Paul Hilken, whose records exposed the operations of a gang of German wreckers implicated not only in the Black Tom and Kingsland blasts but in the firing of ships and the spreading of disease germs. The other was Fred Herrmann, who was located in Chile and finally induced to return to the United States. With amazing frankness, he told of a meeting in Berlin where plans were made for widespread sabotage with Hilken selected to act as paymaster.

Government agents delved deeply into these disclosures. They were still at work when the most startling development of the entire investigation occurred—the discovery of a single piece of evidence that was to challenge the skills of Heinrich in California and bring him to the forefront of the case.

Hilken, rummaging through his attic, had come upon a magazine, brittle and yellowed with age. In it, he said, was a curious message written by Herrmann in Mexico City not long after the United States had entered the war and delivered to him in Baltimore by Herrmann's chauffeur, a man named Gerdts.

The message had been penned in lemon juice across several pages of a copy of the *Blue Book*, dated January 1917, and when pressed with a hot iron the writing became visible, disclosing a cryptic note in which were words and numerals of four digits each.

Working closely with Hilken, the investigators found that by dropping the first digit and reversing the others, page numbers of the magazine were given. On the designated pages names and words had been spelled by the novel device of making pin pricks under letters.

The message, when decoded with Hilken's help, revealed the names of top German diplomats who knew of Herrmann's part in the Black Tom and Kingsland explosions and related his difficulty in getting $25,000 needed to blow up an oil field. It clearly documented the German plot to sabotage American industries turning out war supplies.

Herrmann admitted his authorship and explained the implications of the coded message. There was no doubt but that this was the most crucial individual piece of evidence yet brought to light but to further satisfy themselves of its genuineness, the American investigators located Gerdts, the chauffeur, who admitted delivering it, and found others who had been present when it was prepared.

After much further inquiry, the new evidence was placed before the Mixed Claims Commission to support appeals already filed for a rehearing. It caused an immediate furore among the Germans whose experts examined the "Herrmann Message," as it came to be known, and insisted that it had not been written in 1917 but many years later; in fact, they branded the entire matter as a hoax conceived by Herrmann to benefit the Americans. One of the investigators, with great pride, pointed to several places in paper margins where the writer's pen had penetrated the paper—proof, he contended, that the writing had been done years later when the magazine was old and brittle.

Another of the German experts came forward with another find. He had discovered peculiar check marks in ink opposite titles in the table of contents of the disputed magazine. Believing that these could be used to substantiate their claims concerning the age of the publication, they had scurried through old book shops in New York and found a store on Fourth Avenue with old *Blue Books*—but of later dates—for sale and these showed similar check marks.

Their further inquiry disclosed that the magazines had been sold to the shop in 1930 by the Qualters Brothers in Brooklyn, who readily explained that they were in the habit of making check marks against the titles of articles they had read. This the Germans interpreted as supporting their claim that the magazine with the "Herrmann Message" had been obtained by Herrmann in 1930 or later and that he had faked the message.

The American investigators, however, located the Qualters, who looked at the check marks in the 1917 issue and declared emphatically that these had been made in that year, for they recalled titles of the articles checked.

Charges and countercharges, accusations of trickery and deceit, flew back and forth as it became more and more apparent to the American lawyers and their advisers that their case depended on proving the authenticity of the "Herrmann Message." To do that they would require the most competent and highly recognized experts available and the search began.

It soon became evident that the type of man they needed could not easily be found for it was apparent that the issue would not be decided on handwriting alone but also by incontrovertible judgments on the age of paper and ink; and that the timing of the tiny pin pricks in themselves would be a vitally important factor.

There were handwriting men whose credibility was widely recognized but their performances had been limited to this alone. There were others expert in forensic chemistry. The need was for a man of competency and proven ability in all of these fields, one capable of relating one element of the problem to another. Heinrich's name finally came to the fore and it was agreed that he had won recognition in cases involving disputed documents as well as in others that challenged his laboratory experience as a skilled technician in chemistry and related sciences.

"But he lives in California—on the other side of the country," someone protested. The objection was brushed aside. After much discussion Heinrich was contacted and told of the importance of the case. He agreed to travel East and confer with the American lawyers and government officials.

More than a week later a tall, well-groomed man of middle age, smooth-shaven with sharply chiseled features, walked into an office in New Jersey and presented himself as the scientist from California. When introductions were over, he was shown the aging magazine with its "Herrmann

Message," which already labeled Exhibit 904, was to become the most significantly important piece of evidence in the long and costly legal battle.

Heinrich examined it closely when he was asked if the writing and pin holes could be interpreted in terms of authorship and age, and whether the age of the paper itself could be determined.

"Of course it can be done," he replied, looking over his rimless spectacles, "but it will take time. And I'll be obliged to take this magazine back to my laboratory in California."

"That you can do," he was told, "but are you certain that you can determine not only whether this is Herrmann's writing but when he wrote it?"

"And those pin pricks," a lawyer interjected. "How in the world can you say whether they were made in 1917 or in 1937?"

Heinrich smiled. "It can be done—I've done things like that before. Under the microscope these little holes can be made to reveal their age—a span of years can be detected with surprising accuracy. And, likewise, there are scientific methods for determining the age of paper."

"But what about the ink—the ink used in making those little check marks," another asked. "Once it's on paper, can you really ascertain how long ago it was done?"

Heinrich pulled his fountain pen from his pocket and drew a few straight lines. "The answer is yes," he said, "but my explanation may be a bit technical. Ink, you know, is a solution of a number of things, salts in particular. When it's applied to paper, as I've just done, the solution migrates outward from the point of application, like oil rises in a lamp wick. The paper is porous like the wick and the distance over which this migration has taken place naturally is dependent on the lapse of time. Frequently, the extent of migration can be determined by testing for chlorides or sulphates, or both."

"Just what do you mean by migrating?" one of the attorneys inquired.

"It simply means spreading," the expert explained, always eager to clarify his terms as well as his methods. "Paper, you know, contains hairlike passages which have the effect of producing a suction on the ink, causing it to penetrate further into these passages as time goes on. Have I made myself clear?"

His listeners nodded and after further discussion Heinrich told them that he would need a number of specimens of Herrmann's penmanship made both in 1917 and at the present time. Assured that these would be sent to him promptly, he said that he would return to his Berkeley laboratory, taking with him the disputed Exhibit 904, but first he wished to summarize the issues on which he was asked to pass expert judgment. Enumerated in his usual painstaking way, they involved these basic questions:

Was Herrmann the writer of the message and when was it written—in 1917 or years later?

Were the pin pricks in the paper made in 1917 or years afterward?

Could the Qualters have made the inked check marks in the 1917 *Blue Book* and when were they made?

All agreed that these were the all-important matters for Heinrich to determine and he finally took his leave, advising the group that much time would elapse before he could reach conclusions.

His work began immediately upon his return. In his laboratory with cameras, microscopes, retorts, test tubes, and other equipment he undertook to make pen marks and pin pricks divulge their age, to wring from them mute testimony that would prove or shatter the case of the Americans with millions of dollars at stake.

Many weeks passed before he was ready to present his final report and in the interim he had been obliged to make several trips to New Jersey to confer over questions that had arisen. However, when his findings had been completed, his clients found that this man not only presented his own conclusions, but explained with characteristic thoroughness just how he had reached them. It was one of his customary procedures for which he had received much credit.

In response to his early request for specimens of Herrmann's handwriting, he had received copies of the man's applications for passports in January and June 1915; photostatic reproductions of his letters to the State Department in the same year; and notebook writings over a space of time extending to 1931.

All of these Heinrich had compared with the writing of the "Message" and he declared that he was positive beyond the slightest doubt, that the "Message" was in Herrmann's writing. He had made special effort, he said, to determine whether any of the exemplars had a "date significance" but none was discernible. In all of them, he reported, he had detected evidence of what he termed "slow writing" and this was clearly evident in the disputed lines.

He had spent much time examining enlarged reproductions of Herrmann's writing of the letter "t" in the various exemplars. In these he had discovered variations that first puzzled him, but Heinrich went on to explain in meticulous detail that intricate microscopic study had supported rather than altered his basic conclusions. On this point he wrote:

"This change appears in the writer's treatment of the letter 't' when that occurs at the end of a word. In the older samples of the Herrmann writing, the final 't' is crossed with a short bar, in the standard form. In the later Herrmann writing of the final 't' it is crossed with a swinging stroke which rises from the foot of the stem, passes through it to the left, and then, turning to the right, crosses it again at a suitable height. The resulting form is something like that of an 8."

This form, he found, appeared only rarely in Herrmann's

early writing but never in the "Message." From this he
deducted that had Herrmann been in the habit of using the
8 pattern in his earlier years, it would have appeared in the
cryptic words. To fully substantiate this conclusion, he had
minutely examined the man's writing years afterward and
found the changed "t" construction in use throughout. "In
my opinion," he reported, "the evidence, beyond any justi-
fiable doubt, establishes that the message was written at
the time stated by the writer." This conclusion the Germans never disputed.

Heinrich next explained his tests of the magazine paper
to determine its age and his conclusions not only supported
the American claims but refuted a stubborn contention of
the German experts that pages had been yellowed by the
hot iron passed over the lemon juice writing to make it
readable, rather than by time.

His examination of the inked check marks made by the
Qualters Brothers on the printed pages, and of the paper
itself, convinced him that the paper had become embrittled
with age when the marks were made and that the German
claim of fraud was fallacious. This he further supported by
a study of perforations made by the writer's pen—tiny little
apertures that were almost invisible to the naked eye and
perceivable only under the most powerful lenses.

To the tiny pin pricks he gave still more technical attention, poring over them for days in his laboratory and
examining both sides of the punctured pages under his
microscopes. He carefully pricked papers of varying ages
and compared the little perforations. The final conclusion,
meticulously detailed in his report, was that the holes in the
1917 magazine were made when the paper was new and
definitely were not made in 1931.

Lawyers for the American claimants and government
officials working with them naturally were elated by Heinrich's findings which he further clarified for them on a
special trip to the East. Many questions were asked and

Heinrich spared no effort in explaining the techniques he had used to obtain his results. On one point, however, his listeners told him that they were still confused.

"You've already told us," one of them inquired, "how it is possible to determine the age of ink and of paper. But how can you be so certain that those pin pricks were made when the paper was new and not years later?"

In reply Heinrich took a pin from under his coat lapel and stuck it through a sheet of notepaper. "This pin of course disturbed the infinitely small fibers of the paper," he began, "but the disturbance can be discerned only under a powerful miscroscope—not only on the side through which the pin first passed but on the reverse side, too. With the naked eye, of course, you can see only a tiny hole."

Then he explained that inserting the pin would push the tiny fibers through the hole and that the smoother were the fibers, the older the paper would be. In this case, his study of the fibers had convinced him beyond doubt that the paper was new when the pin pricks were made.

The American authorities, though fully confident of Heinrich's ability, still saw a need for corroboration of his conclusions. Others were called on to check every detail of his lengthy report and his findings received their full approval.

The task of incorporating the report into legal briefs was assigned to Robert W. Bonynge, as agent for the United States, and sheafs of documents were submitted to the Commission.

The result, as already told, was a final judgment written by Associate Justice Owen J. Roberts of the United States Supreme Court acting in the capacity of umpire for the Mixed Claims Commission. It not only reversed the Commission's earlier ruling in Germany's favor but agreed in effect with the American claimants that the Black Tom and subsequent disasters were the work of German saboteurs acting directly under orders of the Kaiser's government.

In consequence awards for damages aggregating $55,000,-000 covered by German funds and securities impounded in the United States, were distributed to those who had suffered losses. Heinrich's work in his California laboratory had won complete acceptance as final conclusive evidence supporting the merits of the American claims.

The case in which Heinrich solved the mystery of the train holdup challenged many of his skills and his wide knowledge of the sciences. Though his work was far different from that involved in the Black Tom affair, many still point to it as one of his many achievements, and some insist that it was even more outstanding than in the other.

The holdup, on October 11, 1923, was as daring as it was foolhardy. Train No. 13 of the Southern Pacific, bound for San Francisco from Oregon, its coaches filled with passengers, was moving slowly through a tunnel in the Siskiyou Mountains in southern Oregon when two bandits, armed with sawed-off shotguns, crawled over the engine tender and commanded both engineer and fireman to stop the train at once.

Sidney Bates, the engineer, and his fireman, Marvin Seng, realizing their predicament, complied just as the locomotive and tender rolled out of the bore. Behind them the mail car was nearly out.

At gunpoint the trainmen were marched to a wooded slope and as they stood with upraised hands they saw a third man running toward them with a bulky package in his arms. This he placed on the side of the mail car and ran.

Bates and Seng still were wondering what to expect when they heard a heavy blast and saw the mail car burst into flames. Only then did they realize that mail robbery was the purpose of the holdup, for the car was loaded with shipments of money, securities and other valuables.

As clouds of smoke billowed from the tunnel, the two

bandits ordered their victims to return to the cab and pull the train completely out of the tunnel. Bates tried to start the engine but it would not move.

With a curse from the robbers, he and his partner were ordered to again leave their posts and they obeyed, reaching the ground just as the brakeman, Charles O. Johnson, came running out of the tunnel, lantern in hand, eager to learn the cause of the train's sudden halt.

At sight of him, one of the bandits raised his shotgun and fired. Johnson fell dead. Two more shots rang out and both engineer and fireman dropped, mortally wounded. The gunmen fled. To the three victims a fourth was added— the mail clerk, Edwin Daugherty, who had been burned to death in his flaming car.

Panicking passengers were quieted with difficulty. In the meantime one of the train crew had telephoned from the mouth of the tunnel to the railroad station at Ashland, Oregon, and in a short time railroad police, deputy sheriffs and other officers were rushing to the scene. Searching for clues, they found a detonating machine with batteries lying on the slope outside the southern mouth of the bore. Its use in setting off dynamite to blow open the mail car was obvious. Near it lay a pair of greasy blue denim overalls and shoe covers of gunny sack soaked in creosote to keep dogs from the scent, and a revolver.

Before long posses were moving for miles in all directions and Daniel J. O'Connell, chief special agent of the railroad, alerted his men at all posts in Oregon and California but there was no trace of the murderous bandits.

As the hunt went on, a deputy sheriff decided to examine one of the batteries attached to the detonating machine and surmised that it might have come from a garage some miles away. Hurrying there with several others, he found a mechanic working alone. His hands and clothes were greasy and someone observed excitedly that the grime looked like the grease on the abandoned overalls. Although he denied any part in the crime, the mechanic was made to try on the pants. They seemed to fit and the young man, still protesting that he was in the garage at the time of the holdup, was taken to jail in a nearby town.

All efforts to link him with the crime were futile and when days passed with no other clues, the officers reluctantly decided to call on Heinrich for assistance, though they were doubtful of what a scientist could contribute.

At Heinrich's request the overalls were sent to his laboratory where he proceeded to examine them inch by inch in his usual methodical way. Scraping off some of the grime, he studied it under the microscope and applied certain chemical tests. Then he dug into a right hand pocket, taking out a few tiny chips and little grains of sand. These he also studied minutely.

A few days passed before those leading the manhunt heard from the man of science. "You are holding the wrong man," he told them over the telephone. "Those overalls were worn by a left-handed lumberjack who has worked around fir trees. He is white, between twenty-one and twenty-five years of age, about five feet ten inches tall, and he weighs about 165 pounds. His hair is medium light brown, his hands and feet are small, and, if I'm not mistaken, he is quite fastidious in his habits. I'd say he has lived and worked in the Pacific Northwest. I'll have more to tell you in a day or two but you'd better send someone down here. I have some questions I want to ask."

The officers looked at each other incredulously, wondering how so much information could be gleaned from only a pair of dirty overalls but their skepticism vanished when they finally listened to his detailed explanation.

"You arrested that mechanic because you thought the grime on these overalls was grease," he began. "It isn't— it's fir pitch. The tiny chips I took from the pocket, enlarged many times under the microscope, prove to be little particles of Douglas fir needles like you'll find in the

Northwest. Caught in the inside hem of the pocket were two or three fingernail trimmings. They had been carefully cut, indicating the man's fastidious habits, and I learned the color of his hair by a single strand caught on a button. Have I made myself clear?"

The others nodded but Heinrich's assertion that the man was left-handed puzzled them. "That isn't hard to tell," the scientist went on. "You see the little fir chips were in his right hand pocket. When a left-handed man chops down a tree, he stands with his right side to the tree and the chips naturally fall into his pocket on that side; but, really, I was able to establish this point in another way—pockets on the left had been used more often than the others and the overalls had been buttoned only on the left."

There were other inquiries and Heinrich answered them obligingly. He explained that it was easy to identify the man as a lumberjack for the overall bottoms had been folded tightly to fit into the tops of boots; the position of the suspender buckles indicated the height and build of the wearer.

"That's all very well," one of the officers interrupted. "But how did you find out that he was a Caucasian?"

"Very simple," Heinrich answered quickly. "I've already told you about the hair adhering to a button. I examined a cross section of it under the microscope. A Caucasian's hair has very definite peculiarities—very different from the hair of an Indian or a Negro, for example."

Heinrich had still another surprise for the officers. He had probed into the pencil pocket of the overalls and found a little piece of crumpled white paper. It was a receipt for registered mail and it bore the notation 236-L. Here was another clue and it proved to be of great value.

Post office inspectors soon ascertained that this was a receipt for $50 sent by one Roy d'Autremont from Eugene, Oregon, to his brother in Lakewood, New Mexico.

Officers hastened north to Eugene where they located

Roy's father, Paul, an aging man, who confided that he was concerned because his sons, Roy and Ray, who were twins, and Hugh had disappeared on October 11, which was the date of the train holdup.

The father described his missing sons and Roy fitted perfectly Heinrich's description of the man who had worn the overalls. And Roy, his father said, was a left-handed lumberjack.

Personal belongings of the trio were taken and sent to Heinrich, who used them to verify his earlier findings. A hair on Roy's brush, examined microscopically, proved to be identical to the single strand found on the overalls button, and the worsted in Roy's sweater matched a short strand found on a towel picked up in a cabin near the tunnel.

By now no one doubted that the d'Autremont brothers were the wanted men but Heinrich continued to produce still further evidence. He had examined the revolver dropped by the holdupmen in their flight. A hidden number on the weapon—763—eventually led to a store in Seattle where it had been sold to a man signing his name as William Elliott.

The register page bearing the signature was sent to Heinrich who utilized his long experience as a handwriting expert and pronounced the writing identical with that of Roy d'Autremont.

A world-wide search for the three brothers now was undertaken with postal inspectors joining railroad detectives and local authorities. Circulars bearing descriptions of the trio and their photographs were printed by the thousands and sent to railroad depots, post offices and police stations throughout the country. Thousands more, in foreign languages, were distributed abroad.

For a time suspects were being picked up in many states and even in foreign lands, for the offer of $15,000 reward had spurred the hunt, but it was apparent that the brothers were safely hidden.

Three years passed until March 1927 when an Army sergeant, Thomas Reynolds, stationed temporarily on Alcatraz Island, then a United States Army depot, scanned the bulletin board in the post office one night and was startled to see the photographs of the wanted men for one of them, Hugh d'Autremont, bore a striking resemblance to a private whom Reynolds had known in the Philippines as Brice. The information was given to the postal inspectors and Hugh was arrested in Manila. He admitted his identity but denied his guilt.

A month later, while Hugh was awaiting trial, the intensified hunt for his brothers ended abruptly halfway across the continent, in Steubenville, Ohio, where Ray and Roy were found working in a steel mill as the Goodwin brothers.

They were taken to the little town of Jacksonville, Oregon, to await the result of Hugh's trial which already was under way. A jury soon found Hugh guilty. His two brothers then confessed and their detailed story of the holdup verified all that Heinrich had disclosed from his study of the meagre evidence.

Hugh likewise admitted his guilt and the three were sentenced to life imprisonment. A pair of grimy overalls, in Heinrich's hands, had proved once more that crime cannot be made to pay.

Chapter 13

Chasing Train Bandits

Daniel J. O'Connell

Pursuing train robbers became a profession for Daniel J. O'Connell during his many years as a detective for the Southern Pacific Railroad. He caught most of them despite cold trails and sometimes without a clue to guide him on his way.

His work was arduous for the Southern Pacific, as the principal passenger and freight carrier in the Western states, became the prey of bandits from the earliest days of its operations. Train holdups had followed the exciting stagecoach era in the West when daring robbers, heavily armed, waylaid the horse-drawn coaches carrying gold from California and Nevada mines to fast-growing cities.

So singularly did the Southern Pacific become the prey of train robbers that it experienced fifty-nine holdups from 1870 to 1933. All but eight were solved and in many cases, especially in later years, O'Connell played the major role, winning national recognition as one of the foremost railroad detectives in America.

Persistence and resourcefulness were the secrets of his success. Working without facilities now common in law enforcement, he had an uncanny ability in uncovering meagre clues and in following them, one after another, until he had achieved his purpose. For him every case was a jigsaw puzzle into which he fitted tiny pieces of evidence until a complete picture of a crime emerged.

He was fearless; sometimes to a fault, as he once demonstrated by capturing the elusive Roy Gardner, a desperate train robber, widely known as "the king of escape artists." Gardner had twice jumped from moving trains while armed guards were taking him to prison. It was in May 1921 while Gardner was being widely hunted for the robbery of a moving train that O'Connell tracked him to a gambling hall in Roseville, California. While the muchly feared fugitive was playing cards with three new-found friends, O'Connell simply walked alone to the table and, taking Gardner by surprise, ordered him to put up his hands. Moments later he led his prisoner away in handcuffs.

While O'Connell always recounted this experience as the most exciting of his career, he is best remembered for his methodical, painstaking efforts in trailing train robbers and his ingenuity in recognizing the value of clues which many would have overlooked as inconsequential.

As chief special agent for the Southern Pacific, the post he filled for a quarter of a century until his retirement in 1944 at the age of seventy, he headed a police force of nearly a thousand men operating through the Western states. For all of them he set an example by his own hard work and methodical ways. They remember him as a demanding taskmaster who was, withal, always fair and understanding—a boss who would not ask any man to do what he himself would not undertake.

Many called him "Hard Rock." It was their way of showing their admiration for the man, his manner and his character, and his stern demands for performance. In no way was it meant derisively.

His successor, William Stone, who became his confidential secretary in May 1925, has his own explanation for the sobriquet. "He was a man a little over six feet tall and he weighed about 195 pounds," Stone recalls. "When I first met him his hair, which had been jet black, was showing signs of graying. He was a handsome man in a very manly fashion. He would glance at you in a very steely manner and perhaps it was that glance as well as his firm ways that earned him the nickname of 'Hard Rock.'"

For O'Connell, however, the road to success was not an easy one. Experience was his teacher and his methods were developed from practice and hard knocks.

Born of poor parents in County Kerry, Ireland, in 1874, he came to the United States as a very young man and started out determined to succeed. Railroading interested him and soon after the turn of the century the Southern Pacific hired him as a trackman. From this, perhaps the lowest rung of the ladder, he rose to foreman.

His ability to handle men and his close attention to duty won recognition. After becoming a railroad police officer, he was advanced to special agent, a post in which he learned much from his Chief, Patrick Kindelon.

O'Connell became his chief assistant and when Kindelon died in 1919, he was appointed his successor, responsible for a wide expanse of territory extending from El Paso, Texas, and Tucumcari, New Mexico, on the south to Portland, Oregon, and as far east as Ogden, Utah.

At all times his work called for crime detection at its highest level. He was a man for detail. He knew the ways of those he hunted and could reckon with their thinking. Modes of operation were carefully cataloged in his mind and when a train holdup or a burglary was reported he would be quick to say "This looks like the work of so and so." Rarely was he mistaken.

He was blunt in reprimanding men for errors, but they accepted his rigorous discipline as his way of teaching them efficiency. When an agent was called into his office and told to stand by the wide oak desk, it was obvious that the Chief was displeased and O'Connell never hesitated to come directly to the point. He rarely praised a man to his face but when he believed an agent's work merited commendation, he made a practice of telling someone else, knowing that the word would be quickly passed to the one concerned.

He is remembered also for his ability to quickly evaluate a person almost on first sight. "There's a man you can trust," he would say, or "he's not reliable, forget him."

"As a police officer and as an investigator he was years ahead of his time," Stone relates. "Things that now have become commonplace, such as the careful, methodical search of the scene of crime, with each item of evidence marked for identification and carefully preserved with proper notations, were not the order of the day forty years ago."

The importance of evidence was always uppermost in O'Connell's mind. Regardless of the nature of the case, he realized that sooner or later—perhaps even after many years—the smallest item might prove a vital factor in a courtroom and that every detail surrounding it then would be essential.

O'Connell's tenacity and rare ability in following one clue after another over a long and twisting road are perhaps best illustrated by his success in capturing two desperate train robbers. It is a case recorded in Southern Pacific archives as an example of his accomplishments in this and other exploits that brought him lasting fame.

At eight o'clock in the evening of March 26, 1932, the company's popular Coast flier, *The Lark,* pulled out of the San Francisco railroad yards at Third and Townsend streets, crowded with passengers bound for Los Angeles. It had not gone far when two masked men, without warning, stepped boldly into the lounge with drawn guns. A moment later fear gripped the startled twenty-five men and women in the car.

The gunmen walked quietly down the aisle to a midway point and stopped. "Get 'em up," the taller of the pair commanded, brandishing his revolver to right and left as' his partner, somewhat nervous, stood guard behind him.

Most of the passengers raised their hands at once but a few, in panic, were slow in complying. "I said up," the gunman barked, "and I don't intend to say it again."

All hands now were up and the bandit, obviously the leader, turned to a man seated at his right, John Horsman. "Take off your hat," he ordered. "Pass it around—and, no funny business."

Horsman obeyed with alacrity and as he moved about with hat in hand, passengers filled it with their money and valuables. He had no sooner stepped back to the robber's side than he felt a revolver barrel pressed against his side. "Now you kick in, too," he was told, and he dropped his wallet into the hat.

The robber then gruffly warned his victims to remain seated and backed into the coach section of the car as his partner followed. "Hey, what about my hat?" Horsman called after him. "Aw, get another one," the bandit snapped.

Passengers in the coach section soon parted with their valuables and the armed men stepped to the vestibule. A moment later they dashed through the car to the forward end where they pulled open the trap door and leaped from the moving train just as it approached a tunnel.

Men in the lounge pulled the signal cord but the engineer, evidently confused by signals in quick succession, decided that there was a leak in the line and continued on his way. Only after the alarm had continued for a time did he stop and then the train was a considerable distance from where the men had jumped.

O'Connell, working in his office late that night, was notified of the holdup and immediately dispatched agents and railroad police to the scene of the getaway. When he arrived a short time later, he found officers searching the ground in all directions. He already had received meagre reports from the crew by telephone together with a fair description of the bandits. The leader, he was told, was the taller of the pair, about forty-five years old and slender. He wore a gray slouch hat, a blue suit, and used a white hand-kerchief for a mask. His partner, described as extremely nervous, was dressed in brown, his face concealed with a blue and white polka-dot handkerchief. Passengers said that he seemed to be about thirty years old and of medium build.

Aside from this information, there were no clues but it was apparent that luck had been with the gunmen, for footprints where they had landed were only inches from the mouth of the tunnel. A jump seconds later would have been fatal.

While search of the area continued into the night, San Francisco police rounded up suspicious characters in response to orders to visit cheap dives and other places frequented by men of dubious character. Roadblocks were set up and many cars were stopped.

Early the next morning O'Connell and city police returned to the place where the bandits had left the train and beat the brush in a renewed hunt for clues. They were almost ready to abandon their search some time later when O'Connell discovered eleven burned matches hidden in the tall grass.

As he examined them closely, it appeared to him that they might explain a strange report that had come a few hours before from a couple living on high ground above the tunnel. These people had reported seeing a few tiny flickers of light near the tunnel long after midnight but the flashes had continued for only seconds and then were seen no more.

This spurred the officers to intensify their search over a steadily widening area and at last one of them, Police Sergeant Peter Heinricks, stepped on something hard. He reached down and grasped a .38-caliber Smith & Wesson revolver.

O'Connell dropped it carefully into a bag and had it taken at once to the police Bureau of Identification to be examined for fingerprints, since in all likelihood it had been dropped by the robbers.

Meanwhile hunt for the pair was extending through California and nearby states. The Southern Pacific posted a reward of $2000 and circulars, bearing descriptions of the fugitives, were printed and distributed. As is common in such cases, suspects were picked up in many localities but none proved to be even remotely connected with the case.

Close examination of the revolver disclosed the absence of finger marks but the experts had observed a number—595345—stamped on both the butt and on the cylinder.

"Our first clue and a good one," O'Connell exclaimed, scanning the report. "This just might get us somewhere."

A policeman snickered, commenting with a note of sarcasm that there were many such weapons in America, but the veteran detective was not disturbed. However, at that moment he could not anticipate the long and devious trail over which that gun would lead him—a trail that would cross and recross the continent many times.

His first step was to send a telegram to the Smith & Wesson factory in Springfield, Massachusetts, giving the number of the revolver and inquiring to whom it had been sold. The response came a day later—the weapon had been shipped with many others on January 21, 1929, to a St. Louis firm, the Shipleigh Hardware Company. It was the first of many leads.

A second message then went to the St. Louis police and he soon learned that the gun had been sold on February 7, 1929, to Harry Clark, a sporting goods dealer of Middletown, Ohio. Again the search crossed state lines.

O'Connell now turned to the authorities in Middletown asking them to contact Clark and when they did the hunt pointed to another man. "Clark sold gun to G. D. Billings this city," was the reply telegraphed to the detective. "Trying to locate him now."

The next message was disappointing. Billings had moved

but he had left a forwarding address, that of his father-in-law named Powell in Winchester, Kentucky. Now the trail shifted southward, only to turn back to Ohio when Billings, located in the southern state, told the police that before leaving Middletown he had sold the revolver to one Charles Profitt.

This man was hard to find but when finally contacted he denied emphatically that he ever had purchased the weapon from Billings. The police stated that they were inclined to believe his statement.

O'Connell was in a quandary, fearing that he was at dead end, but experience had taught him never to fully abandon any possibility. He again contacted the Winchester officers, requesting them to question Billings a second time. This proved futile but the police did come upon a bit of information that they believed might be helpful—the man recently had sent an airmail letter to Otis Powell of 230½ Grand Avenue in Los Angeles.

Now the trail turned abruptly back to California, its starting point and O'Connell telephoned to his Los Angeles office, directing his men there to call on Powell and ascertain the nature of the letter.

Powell, located some hours later, told the officers that he had bought the gun from Billings in Winchester but had pawned it for $6 in Las Vegas, Nevada, while on his way to California.

O'Connell received the news in his San Francisco office with mixed feelings. "We've already tracked that revolver across the country and from Massachusetts to Nevada," he remarked to his secretary, William Stone. "Now it's up to us to find the right pawnbroker in Nevada—but I still think this old gun will lead the way; you'll see."

At his direction Los Angeles railroad agents drove to Las Vegas. Three days later they called O'Connell with important news. They had located the loan office where they learned that the holdup gun with three other weapons had been sold to a customer signing his name as Charles C. Wilson. The sale had taken place on January 16, 1932, exactly sixty-nine days before the train robbery.

"Any line on what this man Wilson looked like?" O'Connell asked one of his agents, speaking over the long distance telephone.

"I'll say," was the quick response. "He's a dead ringer for one of the train robbers—the tall fellow who acted like the leader."

"Can't you get that pawnbroker to tell you more about this man?" O'Connell inquired impatiently.

"I'm sure he can. That's why we're meeting him at his home tonight. He doesn't want to discuss it in his shop."

Late that day came further news. Wilson had come to the pawn shop with two other men who had signed their names to the gun register as Lawrence Harrell and A. F. Harris. Their behavior had aroused the suspicion of the pawnbroker who reported the transaction to the police. They, in turn, had learned that the trio had put up at the Overland Hotel in Las Vegas, the register showing the single notation *Jesse C. Rumsey and party, Long Beach.* The writing was identical with the signature of *Wilson* in the gun register of the pawn shop.

Las Vegas police had learned still more, this time from a garage attendant who told them that the trio had stored a Ford sedan under the name of Rumsey and the records showed its license number.

For the first time O'Connell felt hopeful that the long hunt might be nearing a successful end. Telephoning to the State Motor Vehicle Department in Sacramento, the state capital, he learned that the Ford was registered in the name of Jesse Rumsey with an address in Long Beach, a city close to Los Angeles.

Encouraging progress suddenly came to an abrupt halt when railroad agents discovered that the address given by

Rumsey did not exist. However, they undertook a door to door canvass of the area and it finally brought results in an unexpected way. They had located Rumsey's home but no one was in the house and as neighborhood inquiries continued they came upon an old man who knew more about Rumsey than they had ever hoped to learn from a single individual.

"Sure I know Rumsey," their informant told them. "He came to town from Las Vegas with two friends. Their names? I only know that he called them Larry and Eddie. This Rumsey fellow liked to flash a gun and one day when he was drinking he showed me newspaper clippings about a man who'd held up a train in San Francisco and gotten away with a lot of dough. He boasted that he had pulled the job."

Rumsey, in his cups, had rambled on, bragging about a post office robbery and talking freely about the time he had served in Leavenworth Prison.

O'Connell was elated with the news which thoroughly convinced him that Rumsey must be the man who had purchased the holdup gun under the name of Wilson. Of this there seemed little doubt for Rumsey—or Wilson—answered the description of one bandit and he had boasted of a train holdup. But where was this man now?

More agents were assigned to hunt for him and O'Connell called on post office inspectors for help—something that he often did in cases of this sort. It was a wise move for the inspectors, through sources of their own, learned of an address in Los Angeles where Rumsey had been receiving mail in care of a Charles C. Wilson.

They prepared a decoy letter to Rumsey and sent it by special delivery to the new address with instructions to "deliver to addressee only." The letter was entrusted to an experienced mail carrier to whom they confided the important nature of the assignment but Rumsey still could not be located.

The postman's ring was answered by an elderly man who introduced himself as Rumsey's uncle. His nephew, he said, had left for Las Vegas.

Again O'Connell moved his men to the Nevada city but they were unable to find any trace of Rumsey. Meanwhile a telegram from Missouri threw new light on the suspect.

Acting on reports of Rumsey's talk of train robbery, O'Connell had wired his friend, R. S. Mitchell, chief special agent of the Missouri Pacific, asking him to check prison records for the name of Rumsey. Mitchell replied: YOUR MAN RUMSEY HELD UP ONE OF OUR TRAINS IN 1906; SPENT 15 YEARS IN MISSOURI PENITENTIARY; IN 1921 SENT TO LEAVENWORTH FOR ROBBERY OF STATION AGENT IN CENTRALIA, MISSOURI. PHOTOS AND FINGERPRINTS BEING MAILED.

O'Connell promptly utilized these latest clues. Circulars bearing a photograph and fingerprints of the wanted man were printed and distributed over many states, supplementing earlier ones which merely described the train robbers. There seemed little more to do.

Time passed and O'Connell, more impatient than ever, telephoned to his men in Los Angeles, suggesting that they try a second decoy letter to Rumsey's house. His instructions were followed, the letter being received by the same elderly man who posed as Rumsey's uncle but this time the ruse succeeded through an interesting coincidence. The postman had brought with him another letter. It was addressed to Arthur Rumsey, the uncle, and the mail carrier, knowing of the interest in the case, copied the name and address of the sender in his notebook. The name was Charles C. Wilson.

Though it meant nothing to the postman, he turned his notation over to the inspectors. They looked at the street number and stared at each other in amazement. It was the address of the Lincoln Heights jail in Los Angeles! After O'Connell had been advised of this development, two of his Southern agents, accompanied by police detectives, hastened to the jail and asked for Wilson who, they learned, was serving time for begging.

Slowly a man came shuffling out from the cell tiers, unshaven and in shabby clothes. The officers eyed him eagerly and knew at once that he was Rumsey! The long hunt for the train robber had ended—and in a jail!

Unwilling to disclose their interest on first meeting, the officers told him that they were narcotics agents, suspecting him of peddling. This he vigorously denied and when they suggested that he was an addict, he rolled up his sleeves to prove that there was no evidence of needle pricks. With only little more talk, the agents left the jail to notify O'Connell of their discovery.

"I'll wire you a warrant within an hour," he advised. "Stand by and you can serve it."

In short time the officers returned and took the protesting man to headquarters.

"You're Jesse Rumsey," one of them began, "and you might as well admit it."

"My name's Wilson and you know it," the other snarled. "What's the big idea?"

"Don't give us that," another of the officers snapped, showing him a circular bearing a picture of the wanted man. "That's you and you know it. Come clean—we have a warrant for your arrest on a charge of train robbery. You're the man who held up *The Lark*."

"How y'goin' to prove it?"

"How about this?" the officer demanded, showing Wilson his prison record.

"All right, that's me, but you can't pin that *Lark* job on me," he asserted. "You've got me wrong on that one."

For fully an hour he parried questions but it was apparent that he was weakening. "Okay, you've got me," he finally admitted, "but how in hell did you do it?"

They told him about the revolver and its number and how it had led them on the long and difficult trail. Rumsey's face broke into an ugly snarl. "You know," he told them, "we came back to the tunnel late that night to look for that damned gun but we couldn't find it in the dark. We lit all the matches we had hunting for it, but . . ."

"And now that," interrupted one of the detectives, "explains those little flashes of light that those two people saw from way up on the hill."

Rumsey then related all of the details of the robbery, telling how he had met his partner, Joe Johnson, on a bus traveling to San Francisco from Los Angeles. During the trip they had planned the holdup. Arriving in San Francisco they had gone directly to the railroad depot to check train schedules and finally had selected *The Lark* for their victim.

After the holdup they had sneaked through the railroad yards to a streetcar that took them into the city. Then they boarded a cab and left it only a few yards from Police Headquarters in the Hall of Justice. "We figured no one would look for us around there," said Rumsey. "We found a hotel a block away and who do you think gave me a light in front of the place—a copper."

They pressed Rumsey about his partner but he insisted that he knew little about the man. The two had separated, he said, the day after the robbery when Rumsey left for Los Angeles—on a Southern Pacific train. However, he did give them a fair description of Johnson and the name of his girl friend in Long Beach.

When this woman was located after a day's search, she explained that she could be of little help but she did provide what promised to be a valuable clue. "He's a seaman," she told the railroad agents, "and he usually puts up at those seamen's institutes."

This was enough for O'Connell whose successful pursuit of Rumsey had spurred his determination to land the partner. Hanging up the telephone he started for the San Francisco waterfront and soon was in the Seamen's Institute. There he was told that Johnson had registered on

March 26, the day of the holdup, and had left $90 with the clerk for safekeeping but he had withdrawn his money three days later, stating that he intended to cross the country on a motorcycle.

"By the way," the clerk told O'Connell, "I think he forgot to take his motorcycle registration slip with him. It might just be in my drawer."

The paper was there and it bore the name of Thomas Sifton, a dealer in another part of the city.

O'Connell looked at it and smiled. "I've been chasing an old revolver all over the country," he remarked. "Guess it won't hurt me to start chasing a motorcycle."

Sifton, the dealer, proved extremely helpful. "I won't forget that customer in a hurry," he told the detective. "He was more trouble than the sale was worth."

"Why—what happened?"

"He came in on March 30, picked out a motorcycle, and paid me $70 down," Sifton explained. "He drove it out of here and ran smack into a telephone pole. Then he dragged it back and told me to fix it up—and that wasn't easy. Three days later—that was April 2—I drove it down to the Golden Gate ferry for him. He said he was going to ride to Seattle and come back with it on the boat. Do you know where he is? I haven't heard from him since—and he owes me money."

O'Connell, in turn, explained the situation, wondering whether Johnson had really headed north or had made the statement to deceive the authorities should they pick up his trail. Taking no chances, the detective sent out teletyped orders in all directions, describing the man and calling for his arrest. Then he telephoned to a friend, J. S. Hindman, the Northern Pacific's chief special agent in Seattle, asking him to keep a sharp lookout at the Seamen's Institute in that city and to alert the police. Results came sooner than had been expected.

Late the next afternoon a man walked into the Institute

and lifted a heavy suitcase to the desk. "A fellow named Johnson is calling for this pretty quick," he told the clerk, George Upton, and hurried away. Upton, already on the lookout, eyed the tag, checked the name, and telephoned to the police.

Plainclothesmen arrived quickly, posting themselves in places from which they could closely watch the desk. An hour passed, then two. Finally a tall young man with a ruddy face walked through the lobby and inquired whether a suitcase was being held for a man named Johnson. An instant later the clerk pulled out his handkerchief, his signal to the officers.

With hands on holsters, ready for any emergency, the policemen surrounded the unsuspecting caller and told him that he was under arrest. "What have I done?" he asked, trying to conceal his surprise.

"Come to headquarters with us and you'll find out," he was told.

On the way Johnson evidently realized his plight and admitted his identity. He soon confessed his part in the holdup and explained that his motorcycle had broken down in northern California, compelling him to hitchhike to Washington. "I just thought it would be easier if I shipped my suitcase ahead of me," he said dolefully. "Guess it wasn't so smart after all."

He waived extradition and started on his way to San Francisco. There at headquarters he dictated a confession to which he signed his name. A door opened and in walked Rumsey with a guard. The two train robbers looked bitterly at each other but neither spoke.

Both men were indicted by the grand jury and the police anticipated that they would throw themselves on the mercy of the court but the accused, with nothing to lose, chose to plead not guilty and take their chances with a jury trial.

They were convicted five days later. Johnson was sentenced to an indeterminate term of five to ten years in San Quentin Prison but Rumsey resorted to further legal strategy. Familiar with California law, permitting a separate sanity trial, he pleaded that he was mentally unbalanced, relating that his father had committed suicide and that his mother had died in an asylum.

Alienists appointed by the court undertook a lengthy examination of the man and reported that in their judgment he was feigning insanity. He was sentenced to serve from five years to life in Folsom Penitentiary but Judge Louis H. Ward had something more to say:

"I shall advise the Parole Board that you be dealt with according to your part as the leader of the crime."

Rumsey gulped and was led away.

For O'Connell it was the successful close of another case in which persistence had served the ends of justice.